W9-AFE-797

About Island Press

Island Press is the only nonprofit organization in the United States whose principal purpose is the publication of books on environmental issues and natural resource management. We provide solutions-oriented information to professionals, public officials, business and community leaders, and concerned citizens who are shaping responses to environmental problems.

In 2001, Island Press celebrates its seventeenth anniversary as the leading provider of timely and practical books that take a multidisciplinary approach to critical environmental concerns. Our growing list of titles reflects our commitment to bringing the best of an expanding body of literature to the environmental community throughout North America and the world.

Support for Island Press is provided by The Bullitt Foundation, The Mary Flagler Cary Charitable Trust, The Nathan Cummings Foundation, Geraldine R. Dodge Foundation, Doris Duke Charitable Foundation, The Charles Engelhard Foundation, The Ford Foundation, The George Gund Foundation, The Vira I. Heinz Endowment, The William and Flora Hewlett Foundation, W. Alton Jones Foundation, The John D. and Catherine T. MacArthur Foundation, The Andrew W. Mellon Foundation, The Charles Stewart Mott Foundation, The Curtis and Edith Munson Foundation, National Fish and Wildlife Foundation, The New-Land Foundation, Oak Foundation, The Overbrook Foundation, The David and Lucile Packard Foundation, The Pew Charitable Trusts, Rockefeller Brothers Fund, The Winslow Foundation, and other generous donors.

Better
Environmental
Policy Studies

F.W. Olin College Library

Better Environmental Policy Studies

*How to Design and Conduct
More Effective Analysis*

■

Lawrence E. Susskind
Ravi K. Jain
Andrew O. Martyniuk

ISLAND PRESS

Washington • Covelo • London

F.W. Olin College Library

© 2001 by Island Press

All rights reserved under International and Pan-American Copyright Conventions. No part of this book may be reproduced in any form or by any means without permission in writing from the publisher: Island Press, 1718 Connecticut Ave., N.W., Suite 300, Washington, DC 20009.

Library of Congress Cataloging-in-Publication Data

Susskind, Lawrence.
  Better environmental policy studies : how to design and conduct more effective analyses / Lawrence E. Susskind, Ravi K. Jain, Andrew O. Martyniuk.
      p. cm.
  Includes bibliographical references and index.
  ISBN 1-55963-870-2 (acid-free paper) — ISBN 1-55963-871-0 (pbk. : acid-free paper)
  1. Environmental policy—United States—Evaluation. 2. Environmental policy—United States—Evaluation—Case studies. I. Jain, R. K. (Ravinder Kumar), 1935– II. Martyniuk, Andrew O. III. Title.
  GE180 .S855 2001
  363.7'056'0973—dc21

2001003712

British Library Cataloguing in Publication data available.

Printed on recycled, acid-free paper ✿

Manufactured in the United States of America
10 9 8 7 6 5 4 3 2 1

Contents

Preface

There have been many environmental policy studies conducted since 1970. According to one analysis, the "environment" was the second most frequently studied topic in papers published in political science journals (Palumbo, 1992). One possible explanation for why environmental policy studies have figured so prominently in the public policy literature may be that environmental issues impact us all so deeply. We are all concerned about our well-being; and the natural environment either supports or undermines our very existence.

Although many environmental policy studies are published, arguably, few actually lead to changes in environmental policy. In most policy debates, each side can produce a study containing "scientific evidence" to bolster its position. This leads to great confusion. When dueling experts cite competing studies, public confidence in the value of such research is undermined. This point is illustrated quite clearly in the continuing debate over the risks associated with the use of chlorinated organic compounds in industries such as paper and pulp processing and manufacturing. Advocates for each point of view have substantial technical evidence to back up their claims. Many policy makers, unsure of how to interpret the disagreement among the experts, have backed away from taking any action. This may be the worst possible response.

In order to formulate meaningful and effective environmental policy, scientific disagreement must be taken into account, not ignored. In addition, other ingredients must be factored in as well. This book attempts to show how and why environmental policy studies can and should be organized to ensure the best possible results.

In Chapter 1, the issues at stake are framed using the debate over the risks associated with chlorinated organic compounds. The questions that environmental policy studies must answer are enumerated, and the format of the rest of the book is explained.

Chapter 2 discusses the conventional approach to conducting environmental policy studies, including the steps that are traditionally followed, the usual connection between policy studies and policy making, and the pitfalls of the conventional approach.

Chapter 3 shifts gears and presents what we believe are six particularly successful environmental policy studies undertaken over the past several decades. Based on our interviews with the individuals involved, we were able to isolate several key features that these studies have in common. Each of the studies

- defined a policy problem in a way that was particularly helpful to policy makers,
- described the full range of possible policy responses,
- overcame resistance to change on the part of the relevant regulatory agency,
- provided important opportunities for all statekholders to participate,
- worked to enhance the legitimacy of the particular actions or changes suggested, and
- helped ensure that adequate resources would be available for policy implementation.

These characteristics are explored in some depth.

Chapter 4 focuses on the procedural issues involved in organizing environmental policy studies. Six tasks are identified and discussed with reference to the successful environmental policy studies described in Chapter 3:

- Selecting and using experts
- Shaping the relationship between sponsors and experts
- Choosing the right institutional auspices
- Reviewing policy study results
- Learning from the policy studies
- Setting the ongoing policy research agenda

The chapter concludes with a brief discussion of some of the techniques that can be used to help ensure the validity of the findings of environmental policy studies.

Chapter 5 steps back to take a look at the broader theory underlying the organization of policy studies—from an initial look at systems analysis, decision analysis, and rational choice theory to post-positivist participatory approaches to policy analysis. More recent theoretical notions such as policy networks, the advocacy coalition framework, policy learning, and epistemic communities are also addressed.

Chapter 6 recommends some of the best ways of melding analytical methods, rhetorical methods, and process methods in the design and implementation of environmental policy studies. We revisit the issue of whether and how to regulate chlorinated organic compounds to show how these methods can be blended together.

Finally, Chapter 7 provides a glimpse at several international environmental policy issues: global warming and genetically modified foods/transgenic crops. The difficulties involved in reaching international policy consensus on these and other international environmental policy issues are described, and the importance of international environmental negotiation is emphasized.

A number of individuals have assisted us. Special thanks to Paul Schimek and Kathleen Merrigan, doctoral candidates in the MIT Department of Urban Studies and Planning, who helped identify and prepare the analysis of the six successful cases presented in Chapter 3. Support for conducting these case studies was provided by the Army Environmental Policy Institute and is gratefully acknowledged.

LAWRENCE E. SUSSKIND
Cambridge, Massachusetts

RAVI K. JAIN
Stockton, California

ANDREW O. MARTYNIUK
Cincinnati, Ohio

Better
Environmental
Policy Studies

1

Introduction

SETTING THE STAGE

The scene is the office of an environmental policy consultant who is also a professor at a top-ranking university. As we watch from the sidelines, the professor, hearing the phone ring, answers. We eavesdrop on the conversation.

Professor: Good Afternoon, Congressman Randolph.

Caller: Good Afternoon, Professor. As my assistant explained to you briefly, I have a small problem. I was hoping you could help me. Do you have a few minutes to talk?

Professor: Sure, of course.

Caller: As you probably know, there is increasing concern about the dangers to human health and the environment posed by chlorinated organics. In a speech I gave last week, I mentioned that it might be a good idea to ban or at least phase out all chlorinated organic compounds—a view that is advocated by a range of environmental groups like Greenpeace and the International Joint Commission, a watchdog group for the Great Lakes. I wasn't prepared for the flood of calls I got from industries in my district and constituents upset by my remarks.

Several chlorinated organics, including DDT, polychlorinated biphenyls (PCBs), and chlorofluorocarbons (CFCs), have been banned already or are being phased out. The use of chlorinated organic compounds is linked to increases in cancer rates and endocrine disruption, and they may pose serious risks to embryos and developing fetuses. But a host of arguments against phasing them out have appeared in scientific journals, the popular press, and political discourse. The comments Congressman Randolph heard might have included the following:

- There are nearly 15,000 chlorinated organic compounds used today in various industries including plastics manufacturing, solvents, pharmaceuticals, pesticides, and paper and pulp bleaching.
- A panel of Michigan scientists, convened to review the International Joint Commission's decision calling for the phasing out of chlorinated organic compounds, found that there was "insufficient scientific evidence" to support the claim that chlorinated organic compounds produce environmental and health threats.
- Chlorine accounts for $91 billion of gross domestic product in the United States annually and, directly or indirectly, accounts for 1.3 million jobs.
- Banning an entire class of chemical compounds does not take into account the benefits that may be provided by their continued use.

The conversation continues:

Professor: Very interesting. It sounds like you've gotten an earful! I agree; there's certainly a wide range of opinions on this subject.

Caller: Well, there's a lot more. Many of the people who called claimed that a ban on chlorinated organic compounds would be irresponsible and uninformed. My staff, though, keeps assuring me that there's documentation to prove the dangers posed by these compounds.

I know that we need to balance various interests when reaching a decision on a contentious issue. And the well-being of my constituents, indeed of human health in general, must take precedence over everything else.

So, my problem is that I need credible support for the position I have taken—a position I believe in.

Professor: I see your point. Just how can I be of help?

Caller: I would like you to put together a report indicating that there really is scientific support for my position, namely, that the continued use of chlorinated organic compounds poses a risk to human health and the environment and that a ban or a phase-out makes sense.

Professor: Hmm. I am not sure I can help. And even if I could, I'm not sure that's the right way to proceed. You have already come to a conclusion. If you simply need support for your position, then I'm not the person you need. Be aware, though, that such a report will probably not be any more credible than all the other reports, articles, and studies your staff has already looked at on the other side of the chlorinated organic compound debate.

In my view, merely commissioning one more advisory piece will just waste a lot of money. In addition, the results of such advocacy studies are often misappropriated or misunderstood, thereby making it even harder to get the real facts out.

Caller: So, Professor, what would you recommend that I do?

What should the congressman do? First, like any public official, he'll have to decide whether he is locked into a particular policy position before conducting a full-fledged environmental policy study. He needs to consider, for example, if he would support a ban or a phase-out if he learned that the risks to human health and the environment were minimal while the benefits to industry were enormous (in terms of jobs, availability of new drugs, etc.). Whether that's the case or not, only the right kind of environmental policy study would leave room for that kind of counterintuitive result.

What should the professor do? We have often told callers such as the congressman that, if your mind is already made up, we can't help you. No doubt the congressman could find some consultant happy to produce the report he's looking for. Our goal, on the other hand, is to craft studies that can be used as a basis for sound environmental policy making.

How can such studies be crafted in a charged political context like the one introduced by Congressman Randolph? That is the subject of this book. Among the principal points here is that conventional policy studies are often not up to the task. We begin by pointing out the shortcomings of the conventional approach to preparing environmental studies, particularly at the national level. We then offer a different approach, one that builds on what we think were the most useful environmental policy studies completed over the past few decades. These were studies identified by legislators like Randolph, along with government officials, industry representatives, environmental action groups, and others.

CONDUCTING POLICY STUDIES

Environmental policy studies may be undertaken in many different contexts. At the national level, a study might be requested by Congress when it is considering a new piece of legislation. Government agencies often conduct reviews of their rules and policies as a condition of their funding or in response to a request from the current administration. Regardless of whether the policy is to be carried out at the local, state, national, or international level, the issue may be highly charged, and the policy analyst may find it difficult to be heard among the competing interests at the table. The analyst must fulfill the terms of his or her agreement with the study sponsor (often one of the interests at the table) and yet remain independent and credible. The way in which the analyst factors these complications into study design often makes the difference between having an impact and accomplishing nothing at all.

Successful environmental policy studies help to shape the thinking of key policy workers and give them the confidence that they are doing the right thing, regardless of their initial thinking on the subject. Such studies share certain characteristics in that they

- define the problem in a helpful fashion,
- describe the full range of policy options,
- help to overcome agency resistance to change,
- provide opportunities for engaging interested stakeholders,
- enhance the legitimacy of whatever action follows, and
- facilitate setting resource allocation priorities.

In the case at hand, Congressman Randolph might think he needs only to enhance the legitimacy of particular actions. In fact, the other characteristics are equally important to him. Defining the problem correctly is critical. Is the problem of chlorinated organic compounds a problem of human health? Or is it one of jobs, economic growth, and broader societal benefit? Is it a combination of these factors? Or neither? Does it make sense to look at only one industry such as pulp and paper, or would it be best to look at all industries that use a particular chemical compound?

Second, the congressman thinks he has only two policy options: ban the use of chlorinated organic compounds, or do nothing. There may be other policy options he hasn't considered. For example, it might make sense to do a risk benefit analysis for each compound before deciding whether to ban it.

Third, some agencies may already have positions on the issue. A good environmental policy study should be structured in a way that can soften agency resistance to change.

Fourth, there are a lot of stakeholders who will be affected by a decision concerning the use of the compounds. One goal of a good environmental policy study is to involve these groups in organizing the research effort.

As we have already discussed, there are many studies that have their basis in positions for or against the continued use of chlorinated organic compounds. Yet, as the calls to the congressman's office indicate, these studies are viewed skeptically by people who don't like the recommendations they contain. It is thus crucial that a study enhance the legitimacy of whatever policy recommendations finally emerge; otherwise, the policy study probably isn't worth doing. On the other hand, if it's done right, a policy study can help set resource priorities. For example, should Congress spend money on a risk–benefit analysis for each chlorinated organic compound? Is it desirable to invest heavily in monitoring the impacts of these compounds in the decades ahead?

If the congressman is to have any hope of success, he must be extremely careful when assigning responsibility for the study or selecting experts to help. He needs to choose experts who enhance credibility and who bring a range of backgrounds to the issue. Experts also need to be familiar with parallel research efforts and be willing to seek peer review and advice.

Each consideration should play a role in deciding who should help with an environmental policy study. But there are other considerations as well. A second thing to keep in mind is how the study should be conducted. Options include:

- Engaging a major research organization
- Involving stakeholder groups
- Appointing a commission or task force
- Hiring experts directly
- Doing the study in-house (with a federal agency)

Then, of course, there is the question of how to interpret the study results. In other words, what institutional auspices will be used to analyze and interpret study results to ensure that the American people will learn the most from the study.

Caller: Okay, so what you are saying is that I need to address a series of organizational concerns. I suppose you cover these in your book?

Professor: Well, actually, yes. Look at the fifth chapter when you get the book. I go into some detail about the different tools and techniques of policy analysis. I compare the value of systems analysis, decision theory, and other new approaches to internal stakeholder participation in policy analysis. There may be someone on your staff particularly interested in this methodological discussion.

Caller: Good! At least you're not expecting me to go back to school. Well, that's a lot to think about. I'm not sure I can digest everything you've said. However, I am interested in looking at the book.

Professor: I'll have one in the mail to you this afternoon. Feel free to call if you or your staff have questions.

Caller: Thanks. I'll be in touch. By the way, next time you're in DC, drop by.

If we did give a course for members of Congress, we would use Chapter 6 of this book. It reviews the three basic sets of methods and their advantages and disadvantages:

- Analytical methods
- Rhetorical methods
- Process methods

They have all been used successfully in the past. When problems lend themselves to quantification, the analytical approach may be best. However, if the study is focusing more on possible changes in policy, a rhetorical approach, which focuses on persuasion or advocacy, may be more appropriate. Finally, process methods may be most appropriate when there are fewer stakeholders or where there is a need to build consensus among affected groups.

Our hope is that legislators like Congressman Randolph avail themselves of the real and meaningful contributions that a properly conducted policy study can make. But, as we'll see, that is not the only way a policy study can be sponsored and have an impact. As you read this book, continued reference will be made to the issues raised by Congressman Randolph about a possible ban on chlorinated organic compounds. While we do not offer a complete analysis of the policy options surrounding their particular issue, we try to show how and why a "good" environmental policy study on such an issue ought to be done.

The Conventional Approach to Environmental Policy Studies

As the chlorine controversy described in Chapter 1 suggests, numerous policy studies have been undertaken on this and many other controversial environmental issues. Studies on the same subject often come to widely varying conclusions on the human health and environmental risks posed by chlorine and other substances. Lobbyists, activists, and others have tried to use such studies to sway public opinion and to convince policy makers to take action or not to move forward. Finally, studies of this kind have, in fact, resulted in the adoption of certain national policies which, in turn, have become the subject of additional policy studies. Why so many studies? Why so many different results?

In part, the large number of studies conducted on the risks posed by chlorine and other substances owe their existence to the way in which environmental policy studies are traditionally organized and carried out. The conventional approach to such studies virtually guarantees controversy. In the following sections, the conventional approach to conducting environmental policy studies is reviewed with a special emphasis on the various procedural choices that must be made at each step along the way. Next, the connection between policy studies and policy making is discussed. The chapter concludes with a critical review of the conventional approach to conducting environmental policy studies.

HOW ENVIRONMENTAL POLICY STUDIES ARE USUALLY DONE

The conventional approach appears quite logical and mirrors related activities in other sectors of the business or consulting world. However, as mentioned earlier, the results of this process leave decision makers with the unenviable task of sorting through conflicting findings from which they must derive policy advice. What we call the conventional approach can be viewed as a six stage process:

1. Define the issue and suggest a method of analysis.
2. Choose a consultant.
3. Write a contract.
4. Perform the analysis.
5. Submit a draft report for comment.
6. Produce and disseminate a final report.

As with any other business contract, the individual or group seeking an environmental policy study (to answer a question or support a decision they have already made) first narrows the issue or issues they want to address and then selects a method of analysis. The ultimate conclusion may also be stipulated. This information is then embodied in an offer, or, if the government is involved, a request for proposals (RFP). Results, findings, and recommendations are reviewed before a final report is submitted. Ultimately, a final report meeting the contract requirements is submitted and forms the basis for a decision or a policy choice.

Define the Issue

The issue may be construed as broadly or as narrowly as the sponsor wishes. For example, Congressman Randolph (whom we met in Chapter 1) could define the issue as the desirability of banning the use of chlorine. Alternatively, the congressman might define the issue in terms of limiting or reducing the use of chlorine in a particular industry (e.g., paper and pulp). Or, the congressman might define the policy question in terms of the feasibility of a shift to safer chlorine substitutes to replace the compounds used by industry at present. Methods for defining a problem include back-of-the-envelope calculations, quick decision analysis, political analysis, issue papers, and creation of valid operational definitions (Patton & Sawicki, 1993). These can all be applied by the sponsor to refine an issue (or a conclusion), or by a consultant hired to assist in undertaking the policy analysis that has been requested. The findings may be preordained, particularly if the sponsoring organization has its mind made up in advance, and hires a consultant who shares its bias. It is therefore no surprise that many environmental policy studies, all claiming legitimacy, advocate different, or even opposite, positions by the time they are completed. The outcome is a function of the way the issue is framed at the outset.

Choose a Consultant

An individual or group can be selected to perform the analysis. There are several factors that come into play in making this decision. First, one often seeks the best consultant possible for the money, the tacit trade-off being that an individual who is "better" (e.g., more widely known, more highly respected) will add credibility to the findings and, ultimately, to what is recommended. Often, however, study sponsors tend to favor a consultant whose point of view or leanings are already known. Although such an individual or group may not have as stellar a reputation, they are more likely to produce a report that will be received favorably by the sponsor. Finally, consultants may be selected based on their experience in dealing with controversial policy issues. The sponsor may put a premium on having a consultant who knows how to interact with the press and how to function effectively in the midst of controversy. In many ways, this sort of selection process mirrors the use of scientific experts in civil litigation. The expert would not be hired unless he or she could be counted on to produce findings that supported the position of the hiring party. Thus, as with the framing of the issues, choice of consultant plays a role in generating the disparate results produced by environmental policy studies covering similar issues and using equivalent data.

Write a Contract

The major choices in writing and executing a contract involve expectations of what is to be delivered and at what price. Resources are usually limited; hence, emphasis may be on achieving the desired results (e.g., particular findings or recommendations) at a given price. These constraints ultimately hamper the consultant's flexibility. The consultant is often left with a "take it or leave it" decision.

Perform the Analysis

There are a number of different ways to perform and complete the environmental policy analysis, one of which will be discussed at the end of this section.

Submit a Draft Report

The consultant submits a draft report, including recommendations, for review by the sponsor. Draft reports typically outline the information and analytic methods employed, display policy alternatives and rate them using pre-specified evaluation criteria, and offer final conclusions and recommendations. The draft, along with changes suggested by the sponsor, is sent back to the consultant for inclusion in a final report. Here again, the sponsor usually controls the ultimate findings and conclusions. If they do not comport well with the established position of the sponsor, attempts can be made to "soften" the findings or eliminate objectionable recommendations prior to publication of the final report. Ultimately, the entire study can be abandoned if nothing is salvageable in the eyes of the sponsor.

Produce and Disseminate a Final Report

The consultant produces copies of the final report, which are distributed by the sponsor. Indeed, the sponsor typically controls all dissemination of the findings. If the sponsor is happy with the report, it will be sent to key decision makers in an attempt to promote particular environmental policies or influence decisions that are up for consideration.

Another typical approach to policy analysis may involve completing the following six steps (Patton & Sawicki, 1993):

1. Verify, define, and detail the problem.
2. Establish evaluation criteria.
3. Identify alternative policies.
4. Evaluate alternative policies.
5. Display and distinguish among alternative polices.
6. Monitor and evaluate results.

The study sponsor may already have verified, defined, and detailed the problem before hiring the consultant. In fact, the sponsor may have specified certain conditions in the contract, for example, by defining the scope of resources and data to be used for the analysis. Steps 2 through 5 are more likely to be left in the hands of the consultant. Evaluation criteria are typically established in light of such factors as technical feasibility, political viability, and administrative plausibility. Alternatives can be identified using any number of tools, including surveys, literature reviews, or brainstorming. Then, each alternative must be tested against the evaluation criteria using such techniques as extrapolation, forecasting, and sensitivity analysis. Finally, the various alternatives need to be contrasted so that a recommendation can be made (Patton & Sawicki, 1993).

Monitoring and evaluating results, although included here among the elements of a "complete" environmental policy study, may not be handled by the consultant or analyst; however, in some instances the consultant may be retained to develop implementation guidelines or procedures. If the recommended policy is implemented, the consultant or analyst may be retained to ascertain whether the problem identified earlier has been adequately addressed (Patton & Sawicki, 1993).

THE CONNECTION BETWEEN POLICY STUDIES AND POLICY MAKING

The results of environmental policy studies and, indeed, the results of all policy analyses are considered "policy knowledge." With the "information explosion" experienced over the past several decades (and increasing ease of access to information via the World Wide Web), it is not easy to steer the process of environmental policy making by controlling when and how the results of policy studies are released. In fact, there are indications that the results of policy studies are not used by decision makers to the extent and in the way that their authors and sponsors might prefer (Webber, 1992). If decision makers do not use the results of policy studies to make their decisions, then what, if anything, do they use? Other types of policy knowledge available to decision makers include (Webber, 1992; Lindblom & Cohen, 1979):

- Journalistic reports
- Advice from lobbyists and interest groups
- Discussions with staff members, colleagues, and other decision makers
- Books and periodicals
- Reports and newsletters from universities and research centers

In short, there is a lot of information in addition to the results of policy analyses that constitutes relevant policy knowledge. Policy analyses, however, unlike some of these other types of information, "arrange information into an explanation from which the relationships among the underlying aspects of the policy can be identified" (Webber, 1992). With so much information available, sponsors and producers of environmental policy studies should consider what factors could increase the likelihood of study results being included in the "policy knowledge" considered by a decision maker.

Policy analysts assume that the increased use of "scientific findings" in policy making will result in wiser decisions. Most decision makers are also interested in making wiser policy choices, although the findings of policy studies may not necessarily lead to wiser choices (Weiss, 1978). This paradox is often explained by the "two communities theory," which posits that substantial cultural differences impede interactions between analysts and decision makers (Webber, 1992) and can often cause decision makers to ignore policy study results. This theory, and others like it (e.g., knowledge-specific theories, decision-making context studies, and process studies), attempt to explain the reasons policy analyses are not utilized as much as they might be, but most such theories miscalculate the importance of two key factors. They overemphasize the behavior of individual decision makers; and they underemphasize the importance of the flow and dissemination of policy-relevant information—a process over which decision makers have very little or no control (Webber, 1992). In an attempt to address these shortcomings, Knott and Wildavsky (1980) have proposed "seven standards of utilization," which view knowledge use from a broader perspective:

1. *Reception,* which occurs when the results reach the decision maker
2. *Cognition,* which occurs when the decision maker reads, digests, and otherwise understands the study
3. *Reference,* which occurs if the study has somehow changed the decision maker's preference or worldview
4. *Effort,* which occurs if and when the study influences the action of a decision maker (e.g., fighting for a particular result)
5. *Adoption,* which occurs when the study actually influences policy outcomes
6. *Implementation,* which occurs when adopted policy becomes practice
7. *Impact,* which occurs when tangible benefits to society have been realized

These standards provide a way of understanding how policy knowledge is utilized by individual decision makers and has an impact on the overall policy-making process. Understanding the use and flow of policy knowledge, and particularly the obstacles to using environmental policy studies to shape policy, provides insight into why decision makers often choose not to use environmental policy study results.

The first two standards advanced by Knott and Wildavsky—reception and cognition—are usually met. The other standards, however, are not routinely attained. Did the results of the study help to influence the decision maker's worldview or alter the decision maker's preferences? If they were achieved, but had no impact on subsequent policy, it would not have mattered whether the decision maker had received the results of the policy study at all. If, however, the third and fourth standards have been met, but the resulting policy changes are not consistent with the content of the policy analysis, then other, more subtle, forces are at work.

There are several factors that could account for the third and fourth standards not being met. First, did the right questions get asked? In other words, did the environmental policy study address the problem or situation with which the decision maker was wrestling? It might be helpful at this point to refer back to Congressman Randolph's inquiry into the continued use of chlorine. If the policy study focused on reducing dioxin levels in water around paper pulp mills, but the decision maker was trying to decide whether to ban chlorine use all together, it is likely that the decision maker would pay little heed to the results of such a study. Reception and cognition may have occurred, but reference probably did not.

Second, were the results clearly and concisely presented? The manner in which the results of a study are conveyed can greatly influence their impact on policy making. Although poorly conveyed results may meet the reception standard, cognition probably will not follow. A good example of this is what happened when policy analysts and scientists submitted the results of a ten-year, $500 million study to Congress concerning the effects of acid rain. Study completion was timed to coincide with congressional deliberation over amendments to the Clean Air Act. The study results were presented in twenty-seven technical reports and a three-volume "integrated assessment" which, although they contained lots of useful scientific information, were so dense and complicated that they were very difficult for decision makers to digest. Ultimately, the study had little or no impact on the amendments to the act passed in 1990 (Rubin, Lave, & Morgan, 1992).

Finally, were the findings of the policy analysis convincing? If reception and cognition have occurred, has the study provided the decision maker with a new frame of reference? Assuming the correct questions were asked—namely, that the policy study addressed a problem of great concern to the decision maker—there are several factors that could influence the ultimate impact of the study's findings. These include the reputation of those conducting the policy, the degree to which the results may have been undercut by the biases of the sponsor or the analyst, and the manner in which the study was conducted. If the decision maker questions any of these aspects of the study, the results are less likely to be useful, and other types of policy knowledge are likely to gain in importance. Moving to follow-on steps, adoption, and implementation requires commitment by the decision maker and additional resources. An effective policy study can be a motivating force for adoption and implementation and thus provide tangible benefits to society.

COMMENTS ON THE
CONVENTIONAL APPROACH

Given the many obstacles to the utilization of policy knowledge by decision makers, it is not difficult to understand why so many environmental policy studies are conducted, but so few are utilized.

As previously discussed, environmental policy studies increasingly rely on scientific data and findings that are themselves complicated and often multidisciplinary in nature. The conventional approach to conducting policy analyses can often lead to overuse of complicated data in an attempt to justify a certain position. Invariably, as noted with regard to the report concerning acid rain, such study results are often disregarded and fail to ultimately influence policy decisions.

Reference can also be made to the ongoing debate and numerous environmental policy studies dealing with the continued use of chlorine and its effects on human health that illustrate these points quite well.

When policy studies are "rigged" to satisfy the predisposition of the sponsor or the analyst, they are not likely to have much impact on decision making. When the sponsor is associated with a particular position on an issue, it is difficult to separate the results of the study from the bias of the sponsor. Such studies are usually doomed to having a minimal impact on policy making. In other words, studies that reflect a sponsor's bias may achieve reception and cognition according to Knott and Wildavsky, but they are not likely to achieve the five remaining standards.

This does not mean that a sponsor with a particular position can never sponsor an environmental policy study that will be useful to decision makers. It simply means that extra attention must be placed on dispelling concerns about bias from the outset. This can be accomplished by selecting a policy analyst or consultant in an "arm's length" fashion, giving the analyst flexibility in formulating the problem and selecting a method of analysis. Additionally, such studies often provide assurances that the sponsor was not offered an opportunity to change the results of the study. Absent these minimal steps to ensure disinterestedness, environmental policy studies are probably not worth undertaking. Another way of looking at the factors that influence the impact of environmental policy studies is that the process of conducting such studies is paramount. Although individuals like Congressman Randolph are eager to commission environmental policy studies and want to control the scope and outcome of such analyses, that is the worst thing they can do.

In the next chapter we will examine six environmental policy studies in depth. Each has been identified as an example of an effective policy study by a wide range of knowledgeable observers. We will highlight the process considerations in each case that lent credibility to these studies and increased their impact on policy making.

3

How Environmental Policy Studies Can Be Used Effectively

SIX EFFECTIVE POLICY STUDIES

Many environmental policy studies are prepared each year, but, as discussed in the previous chapters, the vast majority are not used in a meaningful way to make or change policy. What makes one study more effective than another? What studies have truly changed the course of environmental policy?

In order to answer these questions, we interviewed key environmental policy makers and political insiders at the national, regional, and state level. Two dozen strategically placed individuals were selected based on their past involvement in and knowledge about environmental issues and national policy making. An additional fifteen policy makers and analysts were contacted based on recommendations received from the first group. Individuals were interviewed by mail, detailed telephone interviews, and office visits (Schimek & Merrigan, 1994). We asked our interviewees to nominate environmental policy studies they thought were particularly effective. Specifically, we were interested in how a study changed the way they thought about a problem, framed an issue for public debate, or influenced subsequent laws, regulations, or agency behavior.

Six studies were most often mentioned as having the greatest impact. While there is no statistical significance to our selection, we were impressed by the overlap this open-ended method of inquiry achieved. Indeed, each of the studies described here was mentioned numerous times.

And, as we set out to learn all we could about the studies we had selected, it soon became clear that the environmental policy "community" shared our sense that these were, indeed, exemplary. In this chapter, we analyze and evaluate the following six studies to learn what we can about them, particularly what they have in common:

- *Regulating Pesticides in Food: The Delaney Paradox*—by the Board on Agriculture of the National Research Council of the National Academy of Sciences
- *Costs and Benefits of Reducing Lead in Gasoline*—by the U.S. Environmental Protection Agency, Office of Policy Analysis
- *Complex Cleanup: The Environmental Legacy of Nuclear Weapons Production*—by the Office of Technology Assessment
- *Reducing Risk: Setting Priorities and Strategies for Environmental Protection*—by the Science Advisory Board of the Environmental Protection Agency
- *New Farm and Forest Products: Responses to the Challenges and Opportunities Facing American Agriculture (AARC)*—by the Task Force on New Farm and Forest Products.
- *Alternatives for Management of Late-Successional Forests of the Pacific Northwest (Spotted Owl)*—by the Scientific Panel on Late Forest Ecosystems

For each, we will provide a description of the study's history, approach, findings, and eventual impact on policy. Our discussion of study impact includes longitudinal analysis; we show how, over time, these studies led to significant new legislation and how they were used as a basis for implementing environmental policy. We then summarize the "uses" of effective policy studies, drawing upon examples from each case. Finally, we close the chapter with a discussion from an opposing frame, by addressing arguments that challenge our findings drawn from these studies. This analysis leads to our discussion in Chapters 4 and 5 of techniques for organizing studies to enhance their effectiveness.

THE "USES" OF EFFECTIVE POLICY STUDIES

Knott and Wildavsky argue that the true effectiveness of policy studies can be gauged not necessarily from the ultimate outcome of a particular policy decision, but from the various roles or uses the study served (1980) (see also Chapter 2). In the past, the roles and behaviors of individual decision makers have been emphasized while the various processes that aid in the dissemination and diffusion of policy knowledge, particularly when national level policies are concerned, have not. The seven standards of utilization proposed by Knott and Wildavsky take a broader view of the impact of policy studies, allowing judgments concerning effectiveness to be ascertained by looking at uses at differing levels in the policy making process (Webber, 1992).

Our six case studies cover a broad spectrum of environmental issues, from ecosystem management, to pesticide levels in food, to nuclear cleanup. At the time of their release, these studies set the agenda for debate on key issues. Since their publication, several have led to significant new legislation. Most importantly, each was used by environmental managers as a basis for implementing policy. Thus, these six policy studies catalyzed and guided the efforts of federal agencies to handle their environmental responsibilities. A review of these cases reveals six important "uses" of policy studies.

First, these studies have played a critical role in *defining a policy problem in a helpful way*. To define the problem, the authors needed to understand its nature and extent. Important questions that the authors asked were: Why does the problem persist? Who gains and who loses from the problem's existence? Who favors or opposes which solutions or policy options and why?

Just the act of initiating a study can change the way that policy makers and the public view the seriousness and boundaries of a problem. Moreover, a study team legitimizes some and deflates other conceptions of a problem when the team articulates its research objectives, identifies information gaps, frames questions for analysis, and constructs empirical models to generate forecasts. This process can have a major impact on the range of recommendations that agencies, interest groups, or the public view as legitimate. Thus policy studies, when properly organized, can shape congressional debate and public discourse about the direction that governmental action should take. In many instances, effective policy studies can widen or alter commonly held understandings, thereby shifting the agenda for policy reform.

Second, policy studies are invaluable for *describing the full range of potential policy responses to a problem*. A study that thoroughly analyzes the potential impacts of various policy options can generate a new set of legislative or executive priorities, inform public debate, and enhance the understanding of policy makers about which course of action they prefer.

Third, policy studies can help to *overcome agency resistance to change.* In some cases, a study may provide insights into the barriers that retard movement in new directions, and at the same time generate a set of arguments and approaches to overcome these barriers. In other instances, policy studies offer integrated sets of recommendations that respond to anticipated institutional, technical, or financial arguments, thus easing implementation.

Fourth, policy studies can provide important opportunities for *engaging stakeholders in collaborative inquiry.* When stakeholders, included as members of advisory committees or technical review panels, are asked to contribute data or advice regarding the design of new programs, it not only helps to educate them, but also adds credibility to the study process, thereby cultivating support for subsequent action.

Fifth, a thorough policy study can *enhance the legitimacy of a particular action,* and thereby create an unassailable justification for certain recommendations. For example, the use of cost–benefit analysis—together with a discussion of long-term environmental preservation—can elucidate some of the benefits of a new regulation in a way that counterarguments are quickly deflated. Thus research can be used to anticipate the challenges that opposing groups will raise.

Sixth, policy studies can help to resolve conflicting needs and *set resource priorities* in the face of budget constraints. Agencies faced with limited budgets and broad mandates can use policy studies as a vehicle for setting priorities and guiding the allocation of resources and personnel. Policy studies can also clarify the responsibilities of different agencies with respect to competing or overlapping policy jurisdiction.

THE STUDIES AND THEIR "USES"

The Delaney Paradox and Pesticide Regulation

Issue: Regulation of pesticides in food
Sponsor: U.S. Environmental Protection Agency
Responsible Agency: Board on Agriculture of the National Research
    Council of the National Academy of Sciences

The "Delaney Paradox" refers to the dilemma that the U.S. Environmental Protection Agency (EPA) has faced in administering pesticide law, in particular setting tolerances for pesticide residues in food. EPA is required to establish different pesticide tolerances for processed food versus unprocessed or raw food. EPA also applies different approval standards to old versus new pesticides. The resulting mix of standards leaves even the best pesticide policy experts struggling to make sense of the system. The need for an analysis of conflicting standards for pesticide regulation led to the study entitled *Regulating Pesticides in Food: The Delaney Paradox,* produced by the Board on Agriculture of the National Research Council, part of the National Academy of Sciences.

The Delaney clause was a provision of the federal Food, Drug, and Cosmetic Act (FDCA) enacted by Congress in 1958. The clause established a "zero-risk" standard that prohibits all traces of cancer-causing additives in processed food. In 1972, Congress amended the Federal Insecticide, Fungicide, and Rodenticide Act (FIFRA), which governs the pesticide approval process. Unlike the FDCA, FIFRA allows EPA to set tolerances for residues of cancer-causing pesticides in raw foods, as long as the agency demonstrates that the benefits from the use of the pesticide exceed its risks. This means that EPA administrators face conflicting mandates created by the two statutes governing pesticide levels in food—depending on whether they are regulating raw or processed food.

Altogether, EPA is responsible for establishing close to 8,500 tolerance levels. This task is complicated by the conflict between FIFRA and FDCA. In the late 1970s, an EPA decision to strike a compromise on the use of the Delaney clause created even more complications: The agency decided it would rigorously adhere to the Delaney clause when acting on all new pesticide tolerance petitions but would avoid applying it retroactively to older pesticides. This led to problems, since many lower-risk pesticides that would otherwise be substituted for older toxic pesticides failed the stringent Delaney test. The result was that older, higher-risk pesticides, effectively grandfathered by EPA's decision, remained in use longer than they otherwise would have. This situation is similar to industry prolonging the life of less productive and more polluting industrial plants due to more stringent environmental standards for new plants. Economic inefficiencies and more environmental damage result from differential treatment of existing plants and new plants. Ostensibly designed to protect the environment, environmental regulations with "grandfathering" clauses often have the opposite effect.

Analysts observed that the EPA was caught between the conflicting standards of two federal laws; by acting on the dictates of one, it violated either the letter or spirit of the other. These conflicting statutory mandates and related policy challenges provided the impetus for the 1987 study by the National Academy of Sciences.

HISTORY

The Delaney paradox first caught the attention of policy makers during a series of hearings held in 1980–81 by a subcommittee of the House Agriculture Committee. The hearings were chaired by Representative George E. Brown (D-California) and overseen by Staff Director Charles Benbrook, the author of a highly regarded committee report outlining the problems with the Delaney clause. In 1981, the first bill to reform the Delaney clause was introduced (S. 1442). Although no action was taken at that time, it signaled the beginning of a contentious public debate.

In 1985, EPA asked the Board on Agriculture (the Board) of the National Research Council (NRC) of the National Academy of Sciences (NAS) to study EPA's methods of setting tolerances for pesticide residues in food. Specifically, EPA asked the Board to examine the current and likely future impact of the Delaney clause on the tolerance-setting process. Officials of the U.S. Department of Agriculture (USDA) and the EPA framed the basic issues underlying the study in several discussions with NRC staff in early 1984. The initial suggestion for the study came from Orville Bentley, USDA assistant secretary for science and education. EPA assistant administrator Alvin Alm also encouraged the NRC to develop a proposal. A joint workshop was convened by the Board and the Board on Toxicology and Environmental Health Hazards of the Committee on Life Sciences (BOTEHH/CLS), also of the NRC, to discuss whether to undertake a study on the Delaney clause, the issues to be addressed, and the overall goals of such a study. The meeting resulted in the Board submitting a "Proposal for Support" to the NAS, which was eventually funded, in large part by the EPA.

The cost of the eighteen-month study was approximately $625,000. The original proposal stated that funding would be sought from the EPA, USDA, the Food and Drug Administration (FDA), various foundations, and the private sector. Once the proposal was approved, the Board approached EPA for funding to undertake the Delaney study, suggesting that it would help the agency determine a course of action for setting pesticide tolerances. In 1985, EPA formally requested that the Board undertake the study and committed to cover most of the cost.

The Delaney Paradox study was written by the Board. The Board was created in 1983 and is one of ten major units within the NRC. Board members are appointed by the NRC to three-year terms on a rotating basis. The Board is independent of the federal government; however, it generally conducts studies at the request of federal agencies. As a result, the federal government typically funds 85 percent of the NRC's work. When a federal agency is unable to fully finance a study, the Board seeks private support. Industry sponsors are not allowed to provide more than 50 percent of the funding for any given project.

APPROACH

In a typical year, the NRC has more than 1,000 committees with approximately 10,000 professionals who volunteer their time. Rather than conducting its own research, the NRC usually evaluates and compiles research done by others. However, the Delaney Paradox demonstrates that this practice is changing. The NAS insists on two important guidelines for writing and reviewing studies. First, before a study may be submitted for institutional review, all members of the committee must have an opportunity to examine the manuscript to ensure that it reflects a consensus of the members' views. Second, every NRC committee report must undergo peer review by individuals independent of the NRC and the study committee's work. See Appendix A, which contains the NAS guidelines outlined above.

To conduct the study, the Board established a seventeen-member Committee on Scientific and Regulatory Issues Underlying Pesticide Use Patterns and Agricultural Innovation (the Committee) from nominations provided by the Board and BOTEHH/CLS. The Committee included experts in the fields of agricultural pest control, pesticide development, agricultural economics, cancer risk assessment, public health, food science, regulatory decision making, and law.

The Committee undertook three principal tasks. First, it examined the statutory framework for setting tolerances for pesticide residues in food and the operation of the tolerance setting process at the EPA. Second, it developed a computerized database for estimating the impacts of the current tolerance-setting standards on dietary cancer risk and on pesticide use and development. Third, it analyzed the likely impacts of changing these standards.

The Board also initiated important efforts to provide the public with information on the study. An information gathering workshop, open to the public, was held early in the process to assess and better define the basic biological, toxicological, and agronomic issues to be examined. A proceedings volume was prepared, including an overview statement presenting basic facts and findings that had already emerged. In addition, the evening before the study was released, the NAS held a symposium with key policy makers to give them a "heads up" on the study recommendations.

In May 1987, after two years of study, the Board released the *Delaney Paradox*. On the day the *Delaney Paradox* was released, the Board held a press conference and a public meeting to answer any questions about their findings.

The report sold for $19.95 a copy. While the National Academy Press typically prints 500 copies of NAS reports, the demand for the *Delaney Paradox* was great. In total, the publisher sold over 6,200 reports, considered "a very fine showing" for an NAS report.

FINDINGS

The study found "no scientific reason for the law's different treatment of raw and processed food tolerances," and recommended that a consistent negligible risk standard be applied to all food products. Furthermore, the Board recommended that old and new pesticides be subjected to equal scrutiny for meeting this standard. The press covered the study extensively. Within four months of its release, three congressional committees held hearings to explore the implications of the study's recommendations.

IMPACT

In 1986, while the Board was still at work on the *Delaney Paradox,* the FDA discarded the Delaney clause in favor of a negligible risk standard for a certain color additive. As expected, Public Citizen and a coalition of environmental groups filed suit. In October 1987, the U.S. Court of Appeals ruled that the Delaney clause precluded the FDA from applying a negligible risk exemption to color additives. The study affected the positions of each of the parties to the lawsuit and the policy actions that followed.

In October 1988, EPA took the first step in implementing the recommendations of the *Delaney Paradox* by announcing in the *Federal Register* its intentions to change tolerance policy. Several groups, including the American Farm Bureau Federation, adopted policy positions endorsing the study's recommendations and supporting the EPA register notice. EPA administrators understood that the policy was at risk of being overturned by the courts, but they believed it was necessary to move forward in every way possible. In May 1989, the Natural Resources Defense Council (NRDC), Public Citizen, the AFL-CIO, and several individuals filed a petition requesting that EPA revoke eleven food additive tolerances claimed to be in violation of the Delaney clause.

During 1989, several bills were introduced in Congress to implement recommendations from the *Delaney Paradox*. Representative Henry A. Waxman (D-California) and Senator Edward M. Kennedy (D-Massachusetts) introduced the "Food Safety Amendments of 1989" (H.R. 1725 and S. 722), which sought to empower EPA to apply a negligible risk standard for pesticide residues. Other food safety bills were introduced by House Agriculture Committee members as well (H.R. 3292 and H.R. 3153). At year's end, President Bush unveiled the administration's seven-part Food Safety Plan and called for major revisions in FIFRA and FDCA to "eliminate a long-standing inconsistency in the law . . . and establish a negligible risk standard."

Early in 1990, EPA denied most of the NRDC petition and reaffirmed its commitment to a negligible risk standard. The EPA presented draft language to Congress to implement the president's plan, which was then introduced as a bill by Senator Richard Lugar (R-Indiana) (S. 2490). Throughout the next two years, numerous bills seeking to overturn the Delaney clause in one form or another were introduced, but each effort ended in a stalemate. Although the environmental coalition conceded in private that it was time to amend the Delaney clause, it refused to compromise in the hope that the courts would rule against EPA and thereby strengthen the environmentalists' bargaining position vis-à-vis the agrochemical lobby. If the court ruled against EPA, only then would the environmentalists agree to amend the Delaney clause in exchange for other significant improvements in FIFRA regarding environmental protection.

In July 1992, the U.S. Court of Appeals for the Ninth Circuit upheld the strict enforcement of the Delaney clause, thereby striking down the 1990 Bush administration's policy. The court sympathized with EPA's untenable position, but insisted that the Delaney clause was the law of the land until Congress acted to amend it.

In February 1993, EPA administrator Carol Browner announced that the Clinton administration would ask environmentalists and the farm industry to consider changes in the federal law that would overturn the Delaney clause. As policy makers tried to implement the recommendations of the *Delaney Paradox,* stakeholders on all sides agreed that it was just a matter of time before it happened. On August 3, 1996, nearly a decade after the study, President Clinton formally signed the Food Quality Protection Act, which abrogates the Delaney clause and establishes a uniform negligible risk standard for pesticide levels in raw and processed food (*New York Times*, August 4, 1996).

The *Delaney Paradox* continues to be widely used in a variety of arenas. Charles Benbrook, former executive director of the Board on Agriculture, believes that the *Delaney Paradox* is "one of two or three of the most influential reports the NAS did in the 1980s" (Benbrook, 1993).

USE 1: DEFINING THE PROBLEM IN A HELPFUL FASHION

When the Board began work on the *Delaney Paradox,* its members had little idea of their ultimate destination. The first task was the most difficult and time consuming: defining the policy problem itself. The Board spent two years designing an empirical model and inputting data in order to evaluate the tolerance-setting issue. The time invested in careful problem definition paid off; once the computer model was up and running, it took only two months to draw relevant conclusions. Charles Benbrook stresses the importance of defining the policy problem, explaining: "By constructing the study in a sound way, our work led to virtually self-evident conclusions." Benbrook concludes that like the Delaney paradox, many difficult policy questions are "murky," and would benefit from greater attention to problem definition (Benbrook, 1993).

The study's clear focus and definition led to the dramatic conclusion that a small change in tolerance-setting policy could eliminate 97 percent of the health risk from pesticides in food. This information shocked many policy makers who had no idea about the degree to which risk was concentrated in a handful of chemicals. Greg Thies, former staff member for Senator Richard Lugar, says that this revelation helped Congress move forward because the tolerance problem was clarified and narrowed to the point where it seemed possible to solve. Thies claims the study was useful "because it caused us to sit down and say there really is a problem with pesticides in this country, but it's not catastrophic and we can do something about it" (Thies, 1993).

Although the efforts to amend the Delaney clause as recommended in the *Delaney Paradox* took nearly a decade to succeed, policy makers argue that this is not a fault of the study. Janet Hathaway of the NRDC says NAS's role is to educate people about pesticides and identify program failures. Hathaway argues that "success lies in getting the information out," and by this measure the study has been very important (Foreman & Harsch, 1989). Carolyn Brickey, former staff member on the Senate Agriculture Committee shares this view, adding that the study was "very useful in raising some of the issues and concerns that we are now debating" (Foreman & Harsch, 1989).

The study gave birth to more than a dozen legislative proposals. Other legislative efforts have been greatly influenced by its findings. For example, the reauthorization of FIFRA included important new data-gathering requirements that can be directly attributed to the *Delaney Paradox*. Numerous hearings and committee reports have also focused on the *Delaney Paradox,* which is now considered by many congressional staffers to be a necessary "Pesticides 101" book. William Stiles, legislative director of the House Science, Space, and Technology Committee says that "you find many dog-eared copies of those reports on staffers' desks." Stiles believes that the *Delaney Paradox* "probably has done more to shape debate on pesticides and food safety than anything else. The report came out in 1987 and we are still reacting to its various recommendations" (Foreman & Harsch, 1989).

The study's effective problem definition has been extremely useful in spurring additional research. The *Delaney Paradox* brought to light the effects of pesticides in children's diets. Richard Wiles, former Board staff member, reports that "the Delaney report was the seed" that grew into the subsequent NAS effort that focused on dietary risks to children (Wiles, 1993). The *Delaney Paradox* also spurred the USDA to rethink its pesticide research agenda. William Tallent, assistant administrator of the USDA's Agricultural Research Service (ARS) says the study "has had a substantial impact on how we do business here at ARS" (Wiles, 1993). The data compiled in the study motivated many organizations to go back and redo the risk calculations themselves, leading to a constructive debate on research methodology.

Although more than a decade has passed since the study's release, it remains the definitive text for understanding pesticide law and its relation to the food system. Richard Wiles credits the report with putting the issue of risk and its management into the public lexicon. The study is the starting point for anyone concerned with pesticide policy, or as Wiles says, "it's one of those benchmark things; if you don't know what it says, you're not in the ball game."

USE 2: DESCRIBING THE FULL
RANGE OF POLICY OPTIONS

The *Delaney Paradox* provided policy makers with quantifiable consequences of alternative policy options. The Board identified and evaluated four theoretical policy constructs, referred to by Charles Benbrook as "what-if scenarios," to determine which approach to tolerance setting would maximize the availability of useful pesticides while minimizing public health and environmental risks. Scenarios were based on what the study identified as "plausible strategies for EPA to follow," and each was accompanied by extensive analysis. Policy makers were informed of the direct consequences of each scenario as well as the potential benefits and risks associated with adopting each one.

The analysis of policy scenarios using real data accounts for much of the study's success. Richard Wiles argues that this "policy lesson" cannot be overemphasized. He contrasts the *Delaney Paradox* with many other government efforts, noting, "there have been a million reports on [the] Delaney [clause] and a zillion papers—some by the [NAS] but they had no effect at all because they had no data" and were based simply on "moral belief" (Wiles, 1993).

USE 3: HELP OVERCOME AGENCY
RESISTANCE TO CHANGE

The Board's analysis of EPA's data led the members to conclude that database development and control needed to be improved within and among agencies. According to the Board, policies, regulations, and funding constraints that prevented greater sharing and use of data would have to be eliminated.

The federal government has spent millions of dollars developing major databases that aided in the production of tables and graphs but fail to facilitate in-depth policy analysis. Charles Benbrook suggests three reasons for this shortfall. First, agency personnel, fearful of weakening their position by sharing information, are territorial about their data. Second, databases are put together by people who have a relatively narrow set of objectives, which do not usually include policy analysis. As with the *Delaney Paradox,* research teams must often retrofit data back into the database in order to prepare it for analysis.

Benbrook argues for a more coordinated approach to data management. He says that the "policy analysis staff should be involved at every step of the way when federal agencies are building databases," even though their involvement may create conflicts within the agency (Benbrook, 1993). Finally, it is currently difficult to construct databases for use by multiple federal agencies. The study made clear that institutional constraints should be addressed so that agencies can share and work with the same data. For example, pesticide databases needed to be equally accessible to EPA, FDA, and USDA. These recommendations provided a powerful argument for federal agencies to overcome resistance to data sharing.

On a more general level, the study helped to smooth the relations between two rival federal agencies with overlapping jurisdictions. The *Delaney Paradox* defined and coordinated the respective roles and responsibilities of EPA and the FDA regarding pesticide issues. In 1985, the FDA announced that it would not apply the Delaney clause to food or color additives if the risk were under a certain threshold, placing FDA policy in line with EPA policy. The W. K. Kellogg Foundation interviewed sixty policy makers in an effort to evaluate the Board's work. In analyzing the impact of the *Delaney Paradox,* the Kellogg analysts found that the study "helped EPA develop better communications with the FDA regarding the shared responsibility for assuring the safety of the food supply" (Foreman & Harsch, 1989).

USE 4: PROVIDING OPPORTUNITIES TO ENGAGE STAKEHOLDERS

The study engaged stakeholders in three different ways. First, the study provided a new way of looking at the tolerance-setting problem that has allowed stakeholders to abandon old positions for a fresh perspective. This was a deliberate EPA strategy. Jack Moore reports that "there was a belief that a study was a necessary step in moving forward since so many people were already staked out on the issue" (Moore, 1993).

Second, the Board convened a multidisciplinary committee as a way to include a variety of viewpoints. Janet Hathaway says that "it was extremely important that there be a variety of different people, scientists, and writers, to distill all the information" (Foreman & Harsch, 1989). Although a variety of viewpoints were represented, Richard Wiles notes that the Committee did not include any environmental advocates, which he finds to be a typical failing of the NAS that should be remedied in future efforts (Foreman & Harsch, 1989).

Third, the Board designed the study to be accessible to a wide range of readers with varying levels of expertise. It is rare that the demand for an

NAS study exceeds 500 copies, yet over 6,000 copies of the *Delaney Paradox* have been sold. The wide distribution of the study ensures that stakeholders have equal access to information.

The study has been widely used as an important source for stakeholders outside the government. It has had a profound impact on public debate about pesticides and food safety. The media use the *Delaney Paradox* as a source of information to evaluate a wide range of issues concerning pesticides and the food supply. As might be expected, the study grabbed front-page headlines across the country when it was first released. Even now, years later, the media still quote the study. More than 1,000 newspaper and journal articles have cited its findings. *New York Times* environmental reporter Keith Schneider says that he keeps the study within easy reach, calling it the "contemporary equivalent of *Silent Spring*" and saying that it "played a major role in revolutionizing public policy" (Foreman & Harsch, 1989).

Consumers have used the study to better understand the risks associated with eating pesticide-contaminated food. Public awareness of pesticide issues has risen as the media and environmental groups have highlighted the study's findings, leading consumers to demand "safer" food from their supermarkets. Three months after the study was published, Raley's Supermarkets, a billion-dollar food chain in Sacramento, California, hired Nutriclean Laboratory to test for toxic chemicals in fruits and vegetables. Today, at least a dozen multibillion-dollar supermarket chains across the country test for the twenty-eight chemicals listed in the *Delaney Paradox*.

USE 5: ENHANCING THE LEGITIMACY OF PARTICULAR ACTIONS

By using real data to demonstrate the likely impacts of each policy alternative, the study provided executive branch policy makers with an unassailable justification for changing the pesticide tolerance-setting system. Jack Moore, then assistant administrator of EPA for Prevention, Pesticides, and Toxic Substances, says, "Armed with the [NAS] report, we moved forward. You can see the fingerprints of the report all over EPA policy" (Moore, 1993). Moore admits that, to some extent, EPA commissioned the NAS study hoping that it would support a change in the Delaney clause: "People were ready to hear what had been said before but not in such a coherent or prestigious fashion." Moore claims that "the blue ribbon commission approach" gave EPA the backing it needed to move forward and bring about a coalescing of public opinion. Congress has also relied heavily on the *De-*

laney Paradox in drafting and defending numerous legislative proposals. The *Delaney Paradox* has given rise to over a dozen legislative proposals regarding food safety, including the aforementioned Kennedy–Waxman and the Lugar food safety bills. Again and again the study is referenced in Congressional debate. Greg Thies stresses the importance of the study in instigating and shaping several bills including one introduced by Senator Lugar: "We backed ourselves saying the NAS did a complete study on this and we covered ourselves in picking a specific [risk] number in the legislation— something which is rarely done" (Thies, 1993). William Stiles reports that to this day Congress evaluates all pesticide bills based on whether they follow the standard recommended in the *Delaney Paradox*.

Lead in Gasoline and the Reduction of Lead Levels in Ambient Air

Issue: Toxic pollution
Sponsor: U.S. Environmental Protection Agency
Responsible Agency: EPA Office of Policy Analysis

The elimination of leaded fuel in motor vehicles is one of the biggest environmental victories since the founding of the EPA. Ambient air lead levels have been reduced by over 90 percent since 1970. The use of leaded fuel was the largest source of these emissions. Regulation of leaded gasoline began with the Clean Air Act of 1970. Over a decade later, the phase-out of leaded gasoline occurred only after the publication of a policy study entitled *Costs and Benefits of Reducing Lead in Gasoline*.

HISTORY

The Clean Air Act Amendments of 1970 provided the administrator of the EPA broad authority to "control or prohibit the manufacture . . . or sale of any fuel additive" if its emissions (1) cause or contribute to "air pollution which may be reasonably anticipated to endanger the public health or welfare," or (2) "will impair to a significant degree the performance of any emission control device or system . . . in general use." In its effort to comply with this mandate, EPA began examining the use of lead in gasoline. In 1971, EPA initiated regulatory proceedings to phase out the lead in gasoline. Two reasons were given for EPA's action. First, human health concerns were raised. Several studies suggested a strong relationship between the use of leaded gasoline and the level of lead in human blood. The studies found that lead could be absorbed into the body from ambient air and that lead was toxic to the human body. Second, leaded fuel was found to be incompatible with the catalytic converter, a device required on all post-1975 automobiles to reduce hydrocarbon emissions.

As expected, there was significant opposition to any lead phase-out. Powerful refiners, who used lead as a gasoline additive to increase octane, joined together with manufacturers of the lead additives in opposition to all lead restrictions on gasoline. On the other side, several environmental organizations, most prominently the NRDC, pressured EPA to move forward with the phase-out.

EPA issued regulations calling for incremental reductions in average lead content of all gasoline sold over a five-year period. However, several factors conspired to slow EPA's lead phase-out activities. Due to the oil crisis in the late 1970s, President Carter directed EPA to postpone the phase-out until October 1980. The EPA ruling was also challenged in the courts. Consequently, the standard was not put into effect until October 1980.

However, EPA was quick to make the standard more stringent. Four factors contributed to EPA speeding up the phase-out. First, a 1982 EPA survey found that 12 percent of consumers who had catalytic converters designed for unleaded gasoline were nevertheless fueling their automobiles with the cheaper leaded gasoline. This resulted in misfiring that caused significant emissions problems. Second, new studies were generated that further linked leaded gasoline with health problems. Third, the U.S. Court of Appeals for the D.C. Circuit, in a case challenging the provisions of the 1982 lead standards, ruled that available evidence "would justify EPA in banning lead from gasoline entirely." Fourth, alcohol fuel advocates were pushing for restrictions on lead in order to make alcohol more attractive as an octane-boosting fuel additive.

Most important, however, was that the EPA needed a strong policy stand to reestablish the agency's credibility. During the early years of the Reagan administration, the EPA's reputation was shattered due to unethical activities by several political appointees. Professionals within the agency were frustrated and were searching for an issue to restore EPA's reputation as protector of the environment. In 1983, taking a tough environmental stand, EPA issued a final rule tightening the lead limit in gasoline. The rule came as a surprise to the environmental community, which hailed the move as a major victory.

Months later, EPA deputy administrator Alvin Alm noted that the studies on lead in gasoline hinted that an even faster phase-out would further improve air quality and health. Although no one expected EPA to mandate further lead reductions, in September 1983, Alm asked the EPA Office of Policy, Planning, and Evaluation to undertake a cost–benefit study of reducing or eliminating lead in gasoline. Joel Schwartz, an analyst who had worked on the 1982 lead regulation, was asked to provide a "back of the envelope" calculation on the benefits of a total ban on lead additives. When he completed his calculations, Schwartz told Alm that early indications suggested that the benefits of such an action would be more than twice the cost (Schwartz, 1993).

APPROACH

Alm directed the Office of Policy Analysis to undertake a comprehensive lead study. A small team of analysts carried out his orders quickly and quietly. In total, only six staff members contributed to the study, with no more than three people working full time at any particular point. From its inception to the issuance of the final EPA rule on lead, the study lasted a total of eighteen months. The key question for the study team was whether the benefits of an additional lead phase-out would exceed the cost.

The *Lead in Gasoline* study was the first real cost–benefit analysis undertaken by the EPA. In 1981, Executive Order 12991 required all regulatory agencies to prepare a regulatory impact analysis for any regulation likely to affect the economy by $100 million or more per year, but EPA had yet to implement the ruling. Although there were no model cost–benefit analyses upon which to base the lead study, the staff took less than four months to develop a preliminary draft to send to outside experts for peer review. Such a peer review process was unusual at the time. The outside experts included in the peer review were automotive engineers, economists, biostatisticians, toxicologists, clinical researchers, transportation experts, and a psychologist. The staff asked that the review be completed in secrecy. In January 1984, the team refined its analysis and incorporated peer review comments into the final report.

FINDINGS

The resulting study was lengthy and highly technical. It contained the underlying model, a description of the team's methodology, and many charts and graphs. EPA estimated the benefits to be gained from reducing lead in gasoline and categorized the benefits into four major categories: (1) children's health and cognitive effects associated with lead; (2) blood pressure–related effects in adult males due to lead exposure; (3) damages caused by excess emissions of hydrocarbons (HC), nitrogen oxides (NO_x), and carbon monoxide (CO) from misfueled vehicles; and (4) impacts on vehicle maintenance and fuel economy. The analysis was conducted using existing databases. First, EPA modified and enhanced a model of the petroleum refining industry originally developed for the Department of Energy (DOE). Second, EPA used one of its existing health databases that had been constructed for another purpose.

The lead study was released to the public in three stages. First, a draft report was released in March 1984, after six months of staff work. The Senate Committee on Environment and Public Works held a hearing to discuss the implications of the study. In August 1984, EPA formally proposed tightening the lead limit as recommended in the cost–benefit analysis. EPA also indicated that it was considering a complete ban on lead to be enacted by the mid-1990s.

In January 1985, a paper by Joel Schwartz on the health effects of lead on hypertension in middle-aged white men was released. After incorporating these additional impacts, the final lead study was released in February 1985. The following month, EPA issued a final rule that established a new standard for lead in gasoline. It was considered by many analysts to be a radical phase-out. In August 1986, the House Committee on Energy and Commerce released a committee print that supported EPA's controversial lead reduction plan.

IMPACT

As one might expect, industry was not too happy with the proposed lead rule and applied pressure to members of Congress to oppose it. However, the study analyzed so many different scenarios that policy makers quickly came to consider the new lead rule as the only reasonable course of action. The cost–benefit analysis was so clear-cut that industry arguments were quickly dismissed. A document produced by the House Committee on Energy and Commerce cites the study as the key reason behind its members' support for the new lead rule.

The lead study helped establish the credibility of two innovative policy approaches. First, the study represented the first real EPA effort to do a cost–benefit analysis. Despite the environmental community's suspicion that cost–benefit analysis would always work against them, the study actually supported a tightening of the lead standard. This eliminated some of the prejudice against cost–benefit analysis and encouraged EPA to make greater use of it in future policy efforts. Second, the new lead rule made use of a new regulatory approach analyzed in the study's model: It allowed for the trading of pollution rights. EPA was willing to test this approach because the study team had provided the analytical backing to demonstrate that it could be effective. Since its inclusion in the lead rule, emissions trading has been used many times by EPA.

The lead study was used by the agency to justify its lead phase-out rule. It was also used by Congress to evaluate policy options, and over time, by policy makers who sought successful examples of cost–benefit analysis and tradable emissions allowances. Analysts throughout the federal government consistently point to the lead study as the clearest example of a policy study leading to agency action. Joel Schwartz, the study director, says "there was no pressure on EPA whatsoever to do anything about lead" (Schwartz, 1993). The EPA rule on lead is directly linked to the study. The release of the first draft study in March 1984 was followed closely by a proposed rule in August 1984. Release of the final study in February 1985 was accompanied by a final rule in March 1985. By all accounts, the study is the single explanatory factor for EPA's sudden and dramatic lead phase-out.

USE 1: DEFINING THE PROBLEM IN A HELPFUL FASHION

The lead study is a case where analysis clearly preceded agency decision making, and determined the course of the dramatic EPA lead phase-out. The cost–benefit analysis defined the key policy issues for decision makers and, as Weimer and Vining (1989) write, moved the debate "beyond disputes over predictions to explicit considerations of values."

There was no external pressure on EPA to initiate a study on lead or to further phase down its use. This lack of external pressure allowed the cost–benefit analysis alone to define the problem and guide agency action. Joel Schwartz contrasts this with other policy efforts generated by "political heat." In those cases, Schwartz argues that policy analysis is not as important as it was in the lead decision because external pressure "sort of gives you a hint as to what . . . to do and how much" (Schwartz, 1993).

Energy consultant Albert Nichols argues that more cost–benefit analysis should be undertaken before key agency decisions are made. He writes that when cost–benefit analysis is carried out during or subsequent to the development of regulations, "the results usually are not available until most of the fundamental regulatory decisions have been made. At that point, bureaucratic momentum, often coupled with strong external pressures or deadlines, makes it very difficult for the analysis to have much influence" (Nichols, 1985).

USE 2: DESCRIBING THE FULL RANGE OF POLICY OPTIONS

The lead study evaluated a wide range of potential lead standards. This analysis used different assumptions about the impacts various rules would have on misfueling, or using leaded gas with catalytic converters. The possible impact scenarios ranged from the complete elimination of misfueling to no change in misfueling rates. In addition, the study computed net benefits both with and without the estimates of the blood-pressure-related benefits of reducing lead levels in gasoline. The final report presented all of the data generated using different assumptions. Regardless of the particular assumptions about misfueling, and whether or not blood pressure-related benefits were included, the study found that net benefits were maximized with the most stringent of the alternative standards under consideration.

Albert Nichols (1985) notes that the full presentation of data had an important impact on the policy process. He says, "At every major meeting, decision makers were presented with quantitative estimates of the effects of alternative options." Weimer and Vining (1989) also note that the EPA analysts were constantly refining their findings, a strategy they believe is a hallmark of successful quantitative analysis.

USE 3: HELP OVERCOME AGENCY RESISTANCE TO CHANGE

Two factors are cited as important in having eased the way for the implementation of the lead study recommendations.

First, it was important that the study was done internally so that the EPA policy staff was fully cognizant of every decision and assumption made in the model. The staff was then able to answer all levels of questions throughout the implementation stage. Joel Schwartz contrasts this with the frequent agency practice of hiring outside consultants to do most of the policy analysis: "We knew what we were doing as opposed to contracting out for all the policy analysis—the standard thing. When you do that you get a report and you really don't understand the details of what went into things" (Schwartz, 1993). Study team member Jane Leggett agrees: "What the policy office does now is spend lots of money on consulting—we don't have people in-house and we spend most of our time pushing paper and managing the contracts. Spending time on details is really critical if it's going to lead to real action because you have to be able to respond when people raise questions and be able to look at the data and do the analysis in a different way. Consultants aren't privy to those kinds of discussions" (Leggett, 1993).

Second, the study analysts carefully scrutinized the potential arguments that would be raised by opponents to the lead phase-out. Numerous calculations were undertaken to provide analysts with the answers necessary to defend the EPA's approach over others. Weimer & Vining cite the "repeated re-analysis to rule out alternative explanations" offered by opponents as critical. They note that the analysts "drew relevant evidence from a wide variety of sources to supplement their primary data analysis." They also point out that the analysts gave serious attention to possible confounding factors, considering both internal tests (such as subsample analyses and model re-specifications) and external evidence to see if they could be ruled out. As a consequence, opponents of the proposed policy were left with few openings to attack its empirical underpinnings (Weimer & Vining, 1989).

USE 4: PROVIDING OPPORTUNITIES TO ENGAGE STAKEHOLDERS

Due to its particular circumstances, the lead study stands as counter-evidence to public involvement in the study process. In this case, EPA decided that its analysis should be conducted in isolation from stakeholders. Stakeholders were viewed as a threat to the integrity and success of the policy effort, and the study was conducted quickly and in secret. Weimer & Vining (1989) write that Administrator Alm "urged speed in order to reduce the chances that word would get out to refiners and manufacturers of lead additives, the primary opponents of a ban, before the EPA had an opportunity to review all the evidence."

Joel Schwartz and Jane Leggett were both briefed on the political sensitivity of their efforts and the importance of keeping the study behind closed doors. Schwartz notes, "The reason we needed to do it fast was that [Alm] was worried that if word got out that we were working on this, the White House would tell us to stop." Leggett adds, "It was highly political. And this was the first Reagan term and there was still a bias against regulation in general. It was conveyed to me that we wouldn't be able to do the work if it were known . . . and that before we went public with anything we better be very careful about our results." Although the lead study was conducted in secrecy, a draft of the study was subjected to peer review and comment.

USE 5: ENHANCING THE LEGITIMACY OF PARTICULAR ACTIONS

The lead study showed environmentalists that cost–benefit analysis would not automatically discount environmental and human health concerns. Instead, it proved to be a powerful method that supported their goals. Use of this tool allowed the EPA to show that eliminating lead in gasoline was the only reasonable approach.

The study clearly justified the EPA's radical lead phase-out. Robert Bamberger, energy policy specialist at the Congressional Research Service, recalls how no one expected EPA to further reduce lead levels in gasoline and that there was almost no pressure put on the agency in this area. Bamberger recalls, "I remember how surprised I was at the time. The [EPA lead] action was counterintuitive to my expectations" (Bamberger, 1993). Joel Schwartz noted that, although no one was pushing the agency to do something on lead, the study was undertaken. Therefore, the "analysis turned out to completely determine the total form of the regulation in all of its details."

Joel Schwartz argues that the cost–benefit analysis cleared the way for agency action. He said, "It's a lot easier to use cost–benefit analysis than it is to tell people they shouldn't do what they want to do." Not only did it move the EPA administrator to act, but the study was crucial in winning the support of other federal agencies. Leggett (1993) reports, "Even the OMB (Office of Management and Budget) said it was a great study."

Weimer & Vining (1989) write of the importance of the lead study in establishing cost–benefit analysis in policy analysis: "As a society we might very well be willing to sacrifice considerable efficiency to achieve redistributional or other goals, but we should do so knowingly. Introducing efficiency as a goal in the evaluation of policies is one way that policy analysts can contribute to the public good."

USE 6: SETTING RESOURCE PRIORITIES

The ability to share data within EPA and between the EPA and the DOE was critical to the study's success. Agencies often jealously guard their data. This not only makes policy analysis more difficult, it also prevents analysts from developing key insights into existing databases. For example, the EPA policy analysts discovered a strong correlation between high blood pressure in middle-aged white men and very low levels of lead. The agency personnel responsible for the database had not seen the connection between these issues because, as Jane Leggett points out, "If you hadn't asked the question, you would have never found that out."

Much of the success of the lead study can be attributed to a multidisciplinary team approach. But EPA analysts advise that unless current reward structures are altered, there will continue to be infighting within agencies and other disincentives for team research. Leggett laments, "The whole incentive basis of the federal government does not reward team research. There is no incentive for someone to help someone else with a study; if the other branch succeeds, then they are rewarded with more research. It is not in anyone's interest to acknowledge help. You need a manager who is committed to team research despite the disincentives."

The success of the lead study's team approach points to the need to increase efficiency in resource utilization within and between agencies, especially in view of diminishing budgets and personnel. Interdisciplinary cooperation is a more effective way to conduct policy studies that will minimize environmental and health risks to the public.

Complex Cleanup and the Environmental Legacy of the Nuclear Weapons Complex

Issue: Toxic pollution and radiation contamination
Sponsor: Senate Armed Services Committee
Responsible Agency: Office of Technology Assessment

Nuclear weapons production in the United States began during World War II. After the war, the Department of Energy (DOE) was authorized to build and manage nuclear weapons for the military. Fourteen facilities, built mostly in the early 1950s, eventually made up the Nuclear Weapons Complex (NWC). By the 1980s, hazardous waste contamination had become a major public issue, and federal facilities, particularly NWC sites, became a prime target of criticism. Nine of the fourteen sites were placed on the National Priority List for cleanup under the Comprehensive Environmental Response, Compensation, and Liability Act of 1980 (referred to as CERCLA or Superfund). Yet the full extent of the problem and its institutional background remained unknown until the Office of Technology Assessment

(OTA) released its study: *Complex Cleanup: The Environmental Legacy of Nuclear Weapons Production.*

HISTORY

During the 1980s, DOE and other federal agencies released a series of reports examining the environmental status of the NWC. In 1981, the Three Mile Island accident spurred the creation of a DOE task force to assess the safety of nuclear weapons facilities. The report concluded that DOE had insufficient resources to handle NWC safety issues.

In late 1985, DOE began environmental surveys of the facilities. The Defense Nuclear Facilities Safety Board was created in 1988 by PL100-456 to oversee the safety of DOE weapons plants, but some facilities (Pantex and the Nevada Test Site) were excluded from its authority. In that same year, the General Accounting Office (GAO) issued a report recommending that DOE give a complete report to Congress detailing its plans for cleaning up facilities and complying with federal environmental regulations. This report was formally mandated in the FY89 National Defense Authorization Act and was subsequently issued by DOE in January 1989. The report detailed a twenty-year cleanup and modernization plan projected to cost $82 billion.

During the late 1980s and early 1990s, a new series of revelations about environmental contamination at NWC and other federal facilities led to increasing political pressure to clean up the sites. Compounding their public image problems, federal agencies claimed sovereign immunity from EPA or state environmental legislation and penalties. A bill to eliminate federal agency immunity circulated in Congress during 1991 and 1992 and was finally signed into law in October 1992. The political pressure to address environmental concerns at DOE facilities led the Senate Armed Services Committee to request an independent assessment of the problem by OTA, one of several research arms of Congress.

APPROACH

Complex Cleanup was prepared by OTA's Oceans and Environment Program. According to standard OTA policy, the research committee developed a plan for the study, which was then approved by OTA's Technical Assessment Board. The OTA report staff assembled an advisory panel of academics, professionals, and public officials to review the OTA research. Several consultants were hired to perform specific portions of the research. The OTA staff also conducted two workshops: one on health effects and the other on remediation technologies. Participants were drawn from industry, consulting firms, environmental groups, academia, and state and federal agencies. OTA's draft report was submitted for peer review to a larger group of professionals, including many from EPA and DOE.

FINDINGS

OTA found several obstacles to evaluating the technological feasibility of NWC cleanup. The study identified a failure on the part of DOE to collate information on public health risks, as well as a credibility problem arising from the secrecy surrounding plant operations, past environmental problems, and a lack of public participation in decisions. In addition, there was an absence of clear agency goals based on a realistic assessment of costs and environmental impacts. In addition to improved goal setting and data collection, OTA recommended several ways DOE should foster public involvement in NWC cleanup. The study proposed the creation of a national citizen's advisory board, as well as site specific advisory boards (SSABs) for each nuclear weapons production facility. The study recommended that: (1) increased congressional oversight was necessary, (2) independent bodies should address health risks, (3) citizen advisory boards should be set up at each site, and (4) the Nuclear Regulatory Commission, or some new designated body, would be better suited to regulate radioactive waste than DOE.

IMPACT

Testimony from OTA staff about study findings was included in the debate on the 1991 Defense Authorization Act. The act incorporated several of the study's recommendations to improve management of NWC facilities. Two of the recommendations in *Complex Cleanup* were included in the final legislation. First, the act gave authority for overseeing cleanups to the Defense Nuclear Facilities Safety Board, a preexisting body that previously had authority only over operational safety issues. Second, funding was authorized for health assessments to be conducted by DOE for the Agency for Toxic Substances and Disease Registry (an agency in the Public Health Service).

The issuance of the study directly prompted H.R. 5121, introduced on May 7, 1992, by Representative Bill Richardson (D-New Mexico). As recommended in the report, the bill would establish a national citizens advisory board and SSABs for each DOE nuclear weapons facility. The bill did not make it out of the Energy and Commerce Committee. In the Senate, SSABs were included as part of the FY93 Defense Authorization, but

the requirement was dropped in conference in favor of a provision requiring DOE to survey potential mechanisms for public involvement in
site cleanups and make a report to Congress (Govan personal communication, May 21, 1993).

About the same time that OTA was due to release its report, the Keystone Center, a nonprofit science and public policy organization that
provides facilitation services, was preparing a participatory dialogue at
EPA's request to discuss the process of federal facility environmental
management (FFERDC, 1993). The committee assembled by the Keystone Center eventually became a formal advisory panel to EPA, known
as the Federal Facilities Environmental Restoration Dialogue Committee
(FFERDC).

The FFERDC included representatives from federal agencies; state, local,
and tribal governments; and community, labor, and environmental groups.
The committee's efforts concern all federal facilities, not just those in the
NWC. However, DOE sites are a major component of FFERDC's work, and
the newly released OTA report was important in the committee's initial
discussions (Mealey personal communication, March 1993). One of OTA's
primary recommendations, the creation of SSABs, was included in the
FFERDC's Interim Report. The DOE endorsed the recommendation, and
agreed to set up four SSABs (Govan, 1993).

USE 1: DEFINING THE PROBLEM
IN A HELPFUL FASHION

OTA shifted the debate over NWC cleanup from technical feasibility to the
institutional capacity of DOE to manage the problem. The Senate Armed
Services Committee had initially requested that OTA investigate the technological side of environmental problems at nuclear weapons facilities.
The OTA staff was asked to "evaluate what is known about the contamination and public health problems at the NWC and to investigate technological and other approaches to solutions." Although the bulk of the report
resembles an environmental impact statement, the OTA's strongest recommendations concern institutional changes rather than technological applications. While on the one hand recommending better data collection and
goal setting, OTA had to conclude that the current institutional structure
made these changes impossible. OTA's analysis suggested that it is important for environmental policy reports to consider a wider scope of problems than the "client" may initially request.

USE 2: DESCRIBING THE FULL RANGE
OF POLICY OPTIONS

Following the shift in problem definition, the new policy options presented by OTA strongly emphasized process and institutional changes rather than technological changes. The study included a detailed description of three major institutional improvements needed for DOE to manage environmental cleanups. First, DOE needed to set clear cleanup goals. Second, DOE had to establish a system to gather the data required to evaluate possible outcomes. Third, Congress needed to reform DOE's current institutional structure by mandating outside regulation and increased public participation.

USE 3: HELPING OVERCOME AGENCY
RESISTANCE TO CHANGE

The OTA report pinpointed potential obstacles to conducting an effective cleanup within DOE. OTA found that DOE's credibility and capability were major obstacles to solving the cleanup problem. The credibility problem was caused by a past history of secrecy, past failures to prevent or address environmental problems, reluctance to disclose information, and a lack of public participation in either "environmental restoration or waste management decisions." Moreover, OTA found that DOE's cleanup plans did not adequately address these issues.

OTA urged Congress to adopt four measures aimed at improving the credibility of the agency and its capability to enact change. First, Congress should increase oversight of DOE on specific issues such as capabilities of personnel, technology development, and site monitoring. Second, Congress should designate independent bodies to assess public health impacts. Third, Congress should create advisory boards, for each site and nationally, to ensure public participation in cleanup decisions. Fourth, Congress should not continue to let DOE regulate itself with regard to radioactive waste, but should give this function to the Nuclear Regulatory Commission, EPA, or a new body.

One weakness of the report was that it did not include strategies for addressing the political obstacles to institutional reform. Overall, the recommendations have met with varying degrees of success. The public health assessment function was assigned to an existing agency, but funding has since been reduced. The proposal to increase public participation has been taken up by EPA and its FFERDC, which is still meeting to discuss environmental concerns at all federal facilities. The recommendation to establish independent oversight of DOE cleanup plans has not yet been taken up by Congress.

Reducing Risk and Setting Environmental Priorities at the EPA

Issue: Comparative risk assessment of environmental problems
Sponsor: EPA Administrator
Responsible Agency: Science Advisory Board of the EPA

What are the most important environmental problems facing the United States? This is the question that comparative risk assessments tries to answer. By the mid-1980s efforts to reduce smog and point-source water pollution had proved relatively successful. New environmental problems concerning industrial toxics, hazardous waste, and indoor air quality, were emerging. Many of these new problems were less obvious, and their remediation forced large costs on specific parties. At the same time, federal and state governments were attempting to reduce expenditures in all areas, including environmental protection. Thus prioritizing environmental efforts became increasingly important. EPA's Science Advisory Board (SAB) policy study *Reducing Risk: Setting Priorities and Strategies for Environmental Protection* addressed this policy goal.

HISTORY

In 1989, shortly after becoming the EPA administrator, William Reilly requested that the SAB review a 1987 EPA staff report on comparative risk entitled *Unfinished Business: A Comparative Assessment of Environmental Problems.* Reilly had read the *Unfinished Business* report in 1987 and was intent on carrying the analysis of risk to the next step (Reilly, 1991). The earlier report was an attempt by EPA scientists and managers to evaluate EPA programs based on relative human and ecological risk. The report was well regarded within EPA, but had limited impact on public debate or agency priorities (Reilly, 1991).

APPROACH

The *Reducing Risk* study was conducted by the SAB, a standing panel of academic and professional experts in a variety of scientific and technical disciplines relating to environmental problems (Alm, 1991). Reilly reviewed several plans for bringing in outsiders to evaluate the 1987 internal report before selecting the SAB. The Board had 60 members who served two-year terms and more than 250 additional people who served as consultants. In response to Reilly's request, the SAB formed a Relative Risk Reduction Strategies Committee (RRRSC), chaired by Ray Loehr and Jonathan Lash. The RRRSC consisted of thirty-nine scientists, engineers, and managers with expertise in environmental and health problems. The committee was divided into three subcommittees: Ecology and Welfare, Human Health, and Strategic Options. Twelve public meetings were held. Each subcommittee issued a report that was later included as an appendix.

FINDINGS

In September 1990, the SAB released its *Reducing Risk* report. The report made numerous recommendations that have been politically influential. First, the report called for equal attention to both ecological and human health risks, and suggested that a wider range of tools should be employed to reduce these risks, including a greater use of market-based policies. Second, the report stated that national programs outside of EPA's jurisdiction (e.g., those concerning energy and agriculture) should adopt environmental priorities. Third, it called attention to overlooked, relatively high-risk issues such as radon and other forms of indoor air pollution. Fourth, it endorsed the concept of pollution prevention as a risk reduction measure.

In January 1991, Administrator Reilly and Professor Ray Loehr, chairman of the RRRSC, testified before the Senate Environment and Public Works Committee about the SAB's recommendations for restructuring environmental priorities. In March of the same year, Professor Robert Huggett and Professor John Neuhold, both of the SAB, testified before the House Science, Space, and Technology Committee. They reviewed the *Reducing Risk* report and its recommendations, and commented on EPA's budget for research and development.

IMPACT

In contrast to the 1987 report (*Unfinished Business*), the SAB report has guided the restructuring of EPA priorities and shaped debate in Congress. EPA's Pollution Prevention Strategy was based on concepts introduced in the report. In March 1991, Reilly wrote that EPA's "budget decisions already are being guided by the risk reduction principles of EPA's long-term planning process." As a result, the FY94 EPA budget showed a reduction in

Superfund spending and increased spending in higher-risk areas such as water quality and indoor air pollution (Currie personal communication, March 3, 1993).

There have been a series of EPA initiatives that can be directly linked to one or more of the recommendations in the report. These include the establishment of the Environmental Monitoring Assessment Program (EMAP) to gather data on ecological risks; several projects that have used an integrated methodology incorporating both economic and ecological analysis; regulations based on quantitative assessments of risks to species; the establishment of the Office of Strategic Planning and Environmental Data within the EPA; and a new focus on the environmental impacts of agriculture and transportation policies (McGartland personal communication, March 10, 1993).

The SAB report also produced some legislative action. After taking testimony from Reilly and some of the report's authors in September 1992, Senator Daniel Patrick Moynihan (D-New York) introduced a bill late in the 1992 congressional session (S. 2132). Senator Moynihan reintroduced the bill as a first-day bill in 1993 as the Environmental Risk Reduction Act, and again in 1995 as the Environmental Risk Evaluation Act (S. 123). According to the senator, "The bill would put into law the major findings of the 1990 *Reducing Risk* report by EPA's SAB" (Moynihan, 1993; *Congressional Record,* 1995). Although none of these bills became law, the concept of risk reduction has been included in a number of House and Senate initiatives looking at more specific issues such as the reduction of risk of mercury pollution (H.R. 2910).

The report spurred a series of comparative risk analyses directed by state environmental agencies and EPA regional offices. EPA has encouraged all fifty states to do risk assessments. In some ways it has been easier for state agencies and EPA regional offices to follow the report's recommendations than EPA's national office because they are less statute-driven (Currie, 1993). There have been some notable successes at the state level. Washington State, for example, has passed legislation to focus resources on high-risk environmental problems. The state-by-state assessments help make the case for geographic variability in risk assessment; one state may require a very different set of environmental priorities than another.

USE 1: DEFINING THE PROBLEM IN A HELPFUL FASHION

Reducing Risk is a kind of meta–policy study; it attempts to clarify the scope of environmental problems in order to reconcile conflicting agency mandates. The study employed a comparative risk assessment to prioritize environmental problems on the basis of human and ecological risks. Once this was accomplished, the agency had a framework in place to help allocate agency efforts in the face of limited resources.

The study effectively widened the traditional conception of risk. The SAB emphasized the ecological dimension of risk alongside risk to human health. It also examined pending risks such as global climate change, which are primarily ecological but also raise many human health issues. This was a new approach; previously EPA had confined its focus to current and residual risks. Many of the "pending risks" cited in the report are of a greater magnitude than the "current risks" (Currie, 1993).

USE 2: DESCRIBING THE FULL RANGE OF POLICY OPTIONS

The SAB committee argued that ranking risks was only the first step toward reducing them; a clear ranking of risks would then require a broader set of instruments to manage them. The report strongly recommended expanding the regulatory "tool kit" to include economic incentives and information transfers, thus adding to the range of policy options available. While these proposals were not original, they helped to strengthen the growing consensus in favor of more sophisticated environmental policies than the traditional "command and control" regulations.

The report also endorsed the concept of "pollution prevention" as a new tool for environmental problem solving. However, this idea does not completely permeate the report. In fact, SAB committee members had mixed views on the subject, and their lack of agreement is reflected in the subcommittee reports attached as appendices.

USE 3: ENHANCING THE LEGITIMACY OF PARTICULAR ACTIONS

EPA's focus on reducing risk has been influential in restructuring the agency's priorities and shaping debate in Congress. First, it proposed a clear set of risk reduction principles that have, according to one EPA administrator, played a significant role in shaping the allocation of agency resources. Second, the study led directly to several new EPA initiatives, including the establishment of EMAP to gather data on ecological risks, new regulations based on quantitative assessments of risks to species, and the establishment of a new Office of Strategic Planning. Third, the study pioneered the concept of pollution prevention as a risk reduction strategy.

Fourth, testimony about the study's findings by senior EPA officials led Congress to incorporate the study's proposals for restructuring environmental priorities into new legislation. Finally, the report catalyzed similar follow-up studies by state environmental agencies and EPA regional officials. In some cases, these studies have produced state legislation to channel resources into areas identified as high risk.

USE 4: SETTING RESOURCE PRIORITIES

The *Reducing Risk* study defined and clarified agency priorities in the face of conflicting requirements and limited resources. EPA has many statutory responsibilities, but its budget does not provide the funding necessary to meet them all. In addition, many actions affecting the environment are under the jurisdiction of other agencies, such as the USDA or DOE. The report's comprehensive ranking of risks guided EPA in setting its budgetary priorities, and helped the agency promote a set of environmental objectives for other agencies. A total revamping of environmental policy based on comparative risk will take time and require congressional action, but *Reducing Risk* represents the first major step in that direction.

AARC and New Farm Products Research and Commercialization

Issue: Expanding agricultural markets by creating agriculturally based products

Sponsor: U.S. Department of Agriculture

Responsible Agency: Task Force on New Farm and Forest Products

America's farm productivity is so great that the country can more than feed its people. Rather than leave land idle and farmers unemployed, farm advocates and policy makers have promoted the concept of nonfood products since the 1930s. The advantage of nonfood products is that they capture the unused farm capacity without displacing or competing with current food products. The terms *new products* and *nonfood products* are used to describe a variety of crops and processes that expand farmers' markets, such as the use of kenaf for newsprint and the production of biodegradable plastics from corn. In recent years, this issue has taken on a new sense of environmental importance, as new agriculturally based products can replace their petrochemical-based counterparts, thereby reducing toxic by-products in the production process.

The USDA has not been a consistent proponent of new crops and products. Rather, its interest has varied with the ups and downs of the farm economy. The need to establish a coherent and durable policy led the USDA to initiate the New Farm and Forest Products Task Force. The policy study produced by the Task Force, *New Farm and Forest Products: Responses to the Challenges and Opportunities Facing American Agriculture (AARC)*, was a key first step in addressing this contentious issue.

HISTORY

Beginning in 1981, export markets for U.S. farm products declined considerably, as countries like India and China increased their domestic food production capacity. In response to this market downturn, Secretary of Agriculture John Block convened a "Challenge Forum" in 1984 to explore the viability of new product markets for U.S. farmers. The participants at the forum agreed that new products were promising and urged further policy analysis. Block immediately appointed the task force to explore the issue and report back to USDA with a plan for action.

APPROACH

The USDA *Alternative Agricultural Research and Commercialization (AARC)* study was undertaken by the twenty-six-member Task Force on New Farm and Forest Products (Task Force) appointed and partially supported by USDA. Designed to engender a collaborative effort between the public and private sectors, the Task Force included representatives from industry, other private sector organizations, government, and academia. A secretariat was formed within USDA as a liaison to the Task Force. The Task Force held an organizational meeting in Washington, D.C., in June 1985, with subsequent meetings hosted by the Procter & Gamble Company, the Monsanto Company, and USDA.

Because each Task Force member had an organizational sponsor, the costs for the study were shared among the public and private sectors. This allowed the Task Force to operate on a semi-independent basis from USDA. There is no overall estimate of what it cost Task Force members to attend meetings. However, USDA did provide some basic staffing and travel assistance at an approximate cost of $50,000.

The key question before the Task Force was how to entice policy makers into investing the resources needed to make new product development a reality. To do this, the Task Force had to analyze why previous efforts at encouraging new product development had failed. The Task Force's directive was to build on existing studies and to focus on identifying gaps and unmet needs that prevented new products from reaching the marketplace. The Task Force reviewed available new products studies and held a series of hearings across the country to hear testimony from expert witnesses. Once obstacles to new product development were identified, the Task Force developed a legislative proposal for congressional action, an approach that set it apart from previous studies that instead had stressed the importance of new products to agriculture.

FINDINGS

The final report consisted of fifty-four easy-to-read pages and a separate seven-page executive summary. The Task Force described the challenges and opportunities facing policy makers in new product development. It also discussed past barriers to success, including: (1) the structure of USDA, (2) scientific constraints, (3) research spending constraints, and (4) the inability to find venture capital, and recommended national strategies to overcome these barriers. No data analysis or in-depth discussion of the benefits of new products was provided. Overall, the study was light on problem description and heavy on policy recommendations and legislative proposals. It concluded with draft legislation that would establish a new entity for developing new farm and forest products.

IMPACT

The Task Force reported back to the secretary of agriculture in June 1987. The findings of the Task Force study were of great interest to the Congress. Several months prior to the study's release, Senator Tom Harkin (D-Iowa) introduced legislation to increase USDA's efforts in the new products area (S. 970). Harkin was aware that a study would soon be released advocating new products, and while the provisions of his bill differed somewhat from the recommendations of the Task Force, overall it captured the spirit of the AARC's proposals.

Three months after the study was released, Senator Kent Conrad (D-North Dakota) held a hearing to review the findings of the Task Force study. Suzette Dittrich, staff aide to Conrad, reports that the senator "left that hearing very energized and ready to do what the Task Force suggested" (Dittrich, 1993). Less than a year later, Conrad introduced the draft legislation contained within the Task Force study (S. 2413), which ultimately would form the basis for the AARC. In his speech before the Senate, Conrad stressed that his efforts were "based on the strong recommendation" of the study that had "enumerated the road blocks to successful commercialization of new agricultural products and processes" (*Congressional Record*, May 19, 1988). He placed the executive summary of the AARC study in the *Congressional Record* and directly credited the Task Force, saying: "The insights of the task force have been invaluable to me in constructing this legislation" (*Congressional Record*, May 19, 1988).

For two years, Congress debated the issue. Several bills were introduced and hearings were held in both the House and the Senate. The Task Force continued to testify in support of AARC. In September 1989, Senators Conrad and Harkin joined forces, merged their bills, and introduced a new legislative version still referred to as AARC—the Alternative Agriculture Research Commercialization program (S. 1695). Because the USDA did not support the specific legislative proposal included in the study, the USDA developed its own initiative to compete with Conrad's bill. Senator Mitch McConnell (R-Kentucky) introduced USDA's proposal (S. 2419) on behalf of the Bush administration promoting new products and increased research for new products.

At the close of 1990, an omnibus farm bill including the provisions of Conrad's AARC bill was passed by Congress. The committee report accompanying the farm bill described the work of the Task Force study in great detail. Today AARC operates as envisioned by the study. It has an annual budget of $10 million and represents one of the areas of increased spending for agricultural research in recent years. As recommended in the study, the AARC "serves as an advocate, catalyst, coordinator, and cooperative funding source for the development of new farm and forest products." Several congressional oversight hearings have been held to review the progress made by AARC and advocates of new products hope to expand the program considerably.

USE 1: DEFINING THE PROBLEM IN A HELPFUL FASHION

There had been numerous studies on new products prior to the Task Force effort. For example, the National Science Foundation (NSF) wrote a report on the topic that Melvin Blase says, "received reasonable circulation in professional circles." The Council on Agricultural Sciences and Technology (CAST) also produced a report that "was very widely circulated" (Blase, 1993). These reports and others focused on the importance of new products and underscored that the government was missing commercial opportunities in this area.

While these studies were necessary building blocks in making a strong case for new products, they failed to give policy makers clear direction. The Task Force study took the important step of identifying the impediments to new product development and ways of overcoming them. It analyzed why the current USDA structure was incapable of advancing new products and recommended a specific set of policy initiatives to solve these problems.

The Task Force study was more successful than previous studies at pinpointing necessary policy actions because, unlike its predecessors, it examined the full range of issues faced in new product development. Prior studies had focused on the scientific obstacles, or the lack of research funds, or the inability to find venture capital financing. But these efforts were ineffective because, as Melvin Blase (1993) says, "You had these people, each with an area of expertise but with blind spots. They didn't know each other and didn't know each other's problems." The Task Force proposal was able to package policy responses to all these problems into one workable solution, convincing policy makers that new products could emerge from the laboratory and appear on market shelves.

Suzette Dittrich (1993) credits the Task Force with pulling together the disparate pieces of information, and giving lawmakers "the energy and the knowledge to get the job done." Without the study, she says it would have been up to a few staff to figure out the best approach to take and it is uncertain that one would have emerged. Paul O'Connell agrees, and says, "Without the study you would have had the same thing we've had over the past 40 to 50 years in this area. Nobody pulled the thing together before" (O'Connell, 1993).

USE 2: DESCRIBING THE FULL RANGE OF POLICY OPTIONS

The study only recommended one course of action. It explicitly stated that a new entity was needed to promote new products. In this sense, it did not evaluate various policy options. However, the Task Force became the focal point for lively discourse on this topic. The Task Force subsequently was asked on numerous occasions to evaluate legislative proposals and advise congressional actors on the most effective course of action. Paul O'Connell (1993) reports that "the Task Force was a focal point for information." Suzette Dittrich admits that she stayed in close contact with the Task Force members throughout the debate on AARC. She emphasizes that "we used the Task Force as a sounding board in drafting legislation." The existence of the Task Force provided policy makers with expertise and feedback on every step in the process leading to the eventual adoption of the study recommendations.

USE 3: HELP OVERCOME AGENCY RESISTANCE TO CHANGE

The study overcame significant disagreement between the White House and USDA, as well as within the ranks of USDA, regarding the importance of new product research. Paul O'Connell, director of AARC, said that the administration followed the study "closely." The Task Force held an odd status; although USDA appointed its members, it was, as O'Connell observes, "independent but blessed by USDA" (O'Connell, 1993). Agriculture Secretary John Block had high hopes that the study would "generate some lightning" and "boost the development of new products, new product uses, the environment, and refocus on value-added products" (Blase, 1993). According to Task Force member Melvin Blase, Assistant Secretary Orville Bentley had a vision of what might be possible in the new products area, and Bentley constructed the Task Force to rock the boat.

About halfway through the study, the Task Force agreed that the current USDA structure was inadequate to advance new products. It recommended that USDA make major changes in its allocation of research dollars, as well as establish a separate funding entity for new products. According to O'Connell, this "made people involved in production research very nervous" because it proposed "a policy shift" that might affect them adversely. In addition, some administrators did not like the concept of a separate entity that would limit their control. Yet the Task Force was allowed to move forward in the face of this resistance. O'Connell observes that "the Department tried to separate itself from the conclusions," but allowed the study to go forward unimpeded.

The final study did not receive official support from the administration. Blase laments, "By that time poor Orville Bentley had been put in a tough position. OMB had put out the word against any new activity. Bentley had been the father of this effort, but as a spokesperson for the administration, he had to say he did not support the legislation." Still, it was clear that the study's recommendations pleased many within USDA, as well as in the Commerce Department and the National Science Foundation, where much of the new product research had been funded.

It is not clear whether USDA initially set up the Task Force as a way to respond to external pressure by appearing to be taking action on new product development, or as a way to isolate policy analysis from internal turf battles that were preventing the work from getting done. However, in the final analysis, the atypical status and structure of the Task Force allowed it to proceed unencumbered by the disagreements that raged within the administration.

During the study period and through to the final implementation of AARC, the Task Force was active in the political arena. Implementation of the study's recommendations occurred, in large measure, because the Task Force was not content to let its advice go unheeded. Melvin Blase says, "We had proposed legislation but things don't happen just because you propose it. A lesson here is that follow-through is crucial. Some of us had worked in this area long enough that this was a cause for us. We didn't let the effort end with the publication of the report" (Blase, 1993).

Blase describes a process of intense lobbying by the Task Force members including "dog and pony shows on the Hill." He continues, "There were a few days when [we] would decide what staffers needed a visit. Gary and I would just make cold calls. There were one or two instances when we gave formal testimony. But [most] of our actions were [conducted] behind the scenes." Paul O'Connell believes this ongoing effort to build support was critical to the study's success: "The Task Force was always pushing this. It provided a gathering circle for advocates."

USE 4: PROVIDING OPPORTUNITIES
TO ENGAGE STAKEHOLDERS

From the beginning, USDA sought to bring together a wide circle of people to evaluate the new products issue and make recommendations for action. The 1984 Challenge Forum included a broad cross section of industry, farm, and university groups. The Task Force that emerged from the Challenge Forum was similarly composed. Although the backgrounds of Task Force members varied, members did share one important viewpoint. Paul O'Connell observes that "they felt very strongly that this was the direction we needed to go—there wasn't a whole lot of disagreement. The people that were in this group were there because they believed there should be a shift from the production area over to concerns beyond the farm gate" (O'Connell, 1993).

The Task Force members successfully engaged other stakeholders in the debate. Melvin Blase reports that the Task Force held meetings across the country where "we invited a series of people to come before us and make presentations. We ran the meetings like congressional hearings." This out-reach created a ripple effect throughout the agricultural community. O'Connell says before long "there was a real ground swell of support among a cross section of agriculture organizations." According to Richard Bender, staffer to Senator Harkin, "the study process increased interest in the issue and the interest generated congressional action." His office re-ceived a great deal of pressure to do something on new products since, "the general feeling in Iowa—in the press, at Iowa State, and among the corn growers—was that this was important" (Bender, 1993).

It was critical that the government provided a forum for nongovern-mental stakeholders to analyze new products issues. Blase recalls, "I was in-troduced to the policy-making process for the first time. I suspect most of us wouldn't have tried to pull together a set of ideas like this and try to get them heard, and then do the necessary follow-through, if we were only act-ing as individuals or even as small groups."

USE 5: ENHANCING THE LEGITIMACY OF PARTICULAR ACTIONS

The study was important in justifying the development of AARC for two reasons. First, as previously stated, the draft legislation contained in the study was the primary justification for Senator Conrad's legislative efforts. Furthermore, according to Paul O'Connell, the study, with its accompany-ing draft bill, was critical in shaping the debate on AARC: "The report is rather detailed on this issue. It said that unless a new entity is created, we're going to have the same thing that we've had over the last 30 to 40 years" (O'Connell, 1993).

The study also lent credibility and legitimacy to the government's pro-motion of new products within the farming community. Some years prior to the study, farmers in Minnesota had been convinced by government to try planting Jerusalem artichokes. The farmers ended up with no money, crops of weeds, and a reluctance to invest in new crops ever again. This was probably due to a number of factors including the failure of an anticipated market demand for ethanol (used in gasohol) and the possible selection of Jerusalem artichoke varieties not optimally suited to local climate condi-tions (Duke, 1983). Melvin Blase says "once the Jerusalem artichoke scam was exposed, it was talked about all over the Midwest." The study reassured the farm community that new product development could be a viable commercial opportunity.

USE 6: SETTING RESOURCE PRIORITIES

The AARC study helped USDA shift resources toward new product development. Once USDA had the study in hand, it reassessed its budget priorities and reallocated funding to new products as the study had recommended. Melvin Blase says that, prior to the study, USDA "just adjusted the budget headings to make it look like they were doing something" (Blase, 1993). After the study, however, real dollars were shifted into this area.

The Spotted Owl and Ecosystem Management in the Pacific Northwest

Issue: Endangered species and forest management

Sponsor: Agricultural Committee and Merchant Marine and Fisheries Committee of the U.S. House of Representatives

Responsible Agency: Scientific Panel on Late Forest Ecosystems

In June 1990, the Fish and Wildlife Service (FWS) placed the northern spotted owl, a native of Pacific Northwest forests, on the "threatened" species list under the guidelines of the Endangered Species Act (ESA) of 1973. Environmental groups and the timber industry began to take vocal and opposing positions on the issue. Several of the agencies involved in species protection and forest management—the Forest Service, the Bureau of Land Management (BLM), the FWS, and the National Park Service (NPS)—jointly created a panel called the Interagency Scientific Committee to Address the Conservation of the Northern Spotted Owl (ISC), which was empowered to develop an owl conservation strategy. Subsequently, the Department of the Interior (DOI) was also required to develop an owl conservation plan to meet the statutory requirements of ESA.

HISTORY

By May 1991, a series of different plans were "on the table." Working jointly on the problem, the House Agriculture and the House Merchant Marine and Fisheries Committees found that certain basic information was lacking. First, no one knew with any accuracy the range and location of old-growth forests. Second, there was little hard data on the potential environmental and economic impacts of any particular owl preservation plan.

To address these information gaps, the committees turned to four government and academic scientists. The Gang of Four, as they came to be called, were well respected among members of Congress and environmental groups. One of the four, Jack Ward Thomas, had already been the team leader of the Interagency Scientific Committee to Address the Conservation of the Northern Spotted Owl (ISC), the body that had produced one of the competing owl plans. The four scientists presented their initial findings to Congress in July 1991. Their written report, *Alternatives for Management of Late-Successional Forests of the Pacific Northwest (Spotted Owl)*, was submitted in October of the same year.

APPROACH

The Gang of Four decided that the problem was one of ecosystem management rather than only owl preservation. Because species are interdependent, the four scientists presumed that preservation efforts targeting a single species would not be successful in the long run. Furthermore, the scientists observed that as ecosystems deteriorate, many species are simultaneously threatened. Since individual species protection plans were time consuming and generated significant political attention, the Gang of Four redefined the objective of the study as how to determine the best forest management policies given certain overarching public policy objectives.

FINDINGS

In the *Spotted Owl* report, the scientists presented fourteen different policy options, ranging in their objectives from high timber yield to high forest protection. These alternatives covered all of the forest management options already "on the table" and analyzed several new ones as well. Scenarios were also considered for each of three different management options for lands located outside old-growth reserves. For each different scenario, the report presented the associated impacts on old-growth forest maintenance and species preservation. The report demonstrated the changes in timber harvest and regional income associated with each scenario.

IMPACT

At the same time that the Gang of Four's *Spotted Owl* report was published, the Endangered Species Committee, sometimes called the "God Squad," was created to consider exempting some timber sales on public lands despite the spotted owl's mandated protection under ESA. The Endangered Species Committee decided in May 1992 to allow sales in a few areas, but the decision was subsequently overturned by a federal court. During the spring of 1992, forest protection bills based on the Gang of Four's analysis were passed by both the House Agriculture and House

Interior Committees. Neither of these versions proceeded any further in that Congress.

The new Clinton administration convened a "timber summit" in April 1993. Representatives of the stakeholders met in Portland, Oregon, to discuss the issue. The Spotted Owl report became "the standard reference point, the starting point for any discussion," and has provided a menu of options for further action on forest management (Owens personal communication, March 11, 1993). The report shifted the focus of environmental protection from the traditional approach—drawing boundaries on a map or counting trees—to designing integrated strategies to preserve ecosystems (Lyons personal communication, February 1993).

In 1995, Congress passed the Emergency Supplemental Appropriations and Rescissions Act (P.L. 104-19). Section 2001 of this law exempted the U.S. Fish and Wildlife Service from preparing an environmental impact statement under the National Environmental Policy Act (NEPA) to ease prohibitions against the incidental taking of spotted owls on nonfederal lands. Although utilization of Section 2001 has been slowed by litigation regarding its implementation, the so called Timber Rider or Salvage Rider has resulted in additional environmental alternatives analyses and draft rules (FWS, 1996). Against this backdrop, hearings held on March 19, 1998, before the House Subcommittee on Forest and Forest Health indicated that since 1990, the year the spotted owl was designated a threatened species, the area of known habitat has increased each year (U.S. Congress, 1998). Although land has been set aside for the spotted owl in national forests where logging is restricted, litigation continues regarding habitat on nonfederal lands.

USE 1: DEFINING THE PROBLEM IN A HELPFUL FASHION

The Gang of Four argued strongly that ecosystem management would accomplish the overly limited goal of owl preservation. This argument was based largely on ecological principles. As species are interdependent, preservation efforts targeting a single species would not be successful in the long run. In their report, the Gang of Four stated, "We have described the beginnings of a practical 'ecosystem approach' to conserving biological diversity. Nature does things in twos and threes rather than singly. So should we in seeking to preserve or mimic nature" (Johnson et al., 1991).

The argument for a broader problem definition also had a practical justification. As ecosystems deteriorate, many species are threatened simultaneously. It is time consuming for agencies to prepare multiple protection plans for many different species in the same habitat. This problem is magnified when the consequences of forest management for human activities are large enough that each conservation plan generates significant political attention. For Congress, this reality points to the value of avoiding the "endangered species of the month" syndrome (Lyons & Gordon, 1993).

The Gang of Four was able to define the problem broadly in part because they were working for two committees with different species under their respective policy jurisdictions. This gave the scientists the impetus to study the impacts of forest management on a range of species besides owls. For example, they discovered that certain fish species were particularly threatened. In addition, the congressional committees gave the scientists a broad mandate to pursue a "best-science" approach to the problem, wherever it would lead them (Lyons, 1993; Gordon, 1993). In response, the scientists identified a range of forest resource management needs that lay beyond the scope of owl preservation, but are strongly related nonetheless. These needs included such items as information gathering and analysis, watershed restoration, and prescribed burning.

USE 2: DESCRIBING THE FULL RANGE OF POLICY OPTIONS

The authors of the *Spotted Owl* report felt strongly that scientists should not make policy decisions. Instead, they wanted to present the effects of particular policy options on people and the environment. The authors write, "We have provided a sound basis for decisions, given the time and information limits within which we operated. Science (at least as exemplified by the four of us and those who assisted us) has done what it can. The process of democracy must go forward from here" (Johnson et al., 1991). The study analyzed fourteen alternatives and included the impact of each level of ecosystem protection on timber harvest and regional income in its calculations. The wide variety of options in the report made it an effective and credible starting point for further discussion.

USE 3: PROVIDING OPPORTUNITIES TO ENGAGE STAKEHOLDERS

Although the Gang of Four consulted with a wide range of experts, including industry representatives and environmental groups, the final recommendations and results are their own opinions. Stakeholders were not involved in drafting or reviewing the report. In some ways, the lack of constituent involvement was advantageous for this kind of policy study. The scientists' well-known professional reputations helped to give the report credibility in the eyes of stakeholders and members of Congress.

USE 4: ENHANCING THE LEGITIMACY OF PARTICULAR ACTIONS

Before the study, Congress was at an impasse due to divided public opinion and a lack of hard data on the potential environmental and economic effects of different strategies. The Gang of Four's report has been called "a watershed event in terms of quantifying the issues and the choices that would have to be made" by Representative George Miller (D-California), chair of the Interior Committee. The study's thorough analysis prompted action by congressional committees and gave them a credible and scientifically sound analysis to justify their policy choices. The two congressional committees that commissioned the study used it as the basis for a new legislative initiative to protect the northern spotted owl.

The scientists felt that it was important to move the debate away from the traditional arguments that pitted owls against jobs or square miles of owl habitat against board feet of lumber. Environmental groups were initially skeptical of this undertaking, in part because some of the scientists had government positions. However, they were generally pleased with the report's conclusions (Owens, 1993). The lumber industry, on the other hand, was critical of the study's results. Despite the Gang of Four's desire to minimize the polarization of different stakeholder groups, much of the continuing debate on the subject pits industry against environmentalists.

USE 5: SETTING RESOURCE PRIORITIES

The report shifted the focus of policy analysis and resource allocation from individual species protection to integrated ecosystem management. Even though the debate surrounding reauthorization of the Endangered Species Act is heating up again, the focus on integrated ecological management is very much in place. The policy study addressed the prior lack of coordination among agencies responsible for protecting endangered species and managing forest resources. The scientists broadened the scope of their initial mandate from devising a plan for protecting a single species to developing a range of strategies for managing forest ecosystems as a whole. They argued that it simply did not make sense for preservation efforts to focus exclusively on particular species. Such an approach multiplied the work of agencies developing species conservation plans while ignoring the fundamental interdependence of ecosystems. To correct this inefficiency, the report provided information and analysis useful to all of the agencies with overlapping responsibilities for forest management.

THE CHALLENGES

The six policy studies discussed in this chapter were identified by decision makers and policy insiders at the national, regional, and state level as being particularly effective. Once we identified these studies, we looked longitudinally at their impact. We can understand why some might challenge our assertion that these were particularly effective. After all, without tangible evidence to show that these six policy studies produced desirable outcomes (i.e., substantive environmental improvements), how can we say they were effective? This is a difficult challenge since we do not have the necessary evidence to demonstrate that the outcomes in each instance were desirable, or that the public policies in question (and not other factors operating independently) produced the intended results. The fact is, there is no evidence to show that the results of these policy-making efforts were consistent with what was envisioned, or that what was envisioned was, in retrospect, desirable. All we can say is that these studies helped to provoke subsequent changes in policy. We cannot prove that these changes were ideal. Our definition of effective focuses more on the process of policy making than on the impacts of the policies themselves.

We can, however, confirm what we had previously theorized about the uses of environmental policy studies; namely, that they can help to shape public debate, bring stakeholders into the conversation, suggest new policy options, enhance the legitimacy of whatever actions are subsequently taken, or clarify resource allocation policies (to help ensure implementation). We are not asserting, however, that all effective environmental policy studies always lead to the results envisioned by their advocates, or that the outcomes of effective policy-making efforts are always cost-effective or even desirable.

Most policy studies probably bolster the technical basis for the political arguments that those in power were inclined to make anyway. Effective environmental policy studies rarely force decision makers to change their views. They may, though, allow certain decision makers to hold their views more comfortably or, in rare instances, force those with opposing predispositions to hold their political fire.

The media play a role in focusing public attention or shaping public opinion about proposed environmental policy changes. Media reaction may well be an important factor in explaining changes in environmental policy. There may be other factors that come into play as well, but even if we have not isolated all the factors that do play a role in shaping environmental policy-making efforts, the important point here is that the six studies we present were indeed effective in influencing public policy making.

Why do the uses or effectiveness of environmental policy studies matter when ultimately public policy decisions are implemented by "fixers"— political figures with the clout to reshape environmental policy during implementation (Bardach, 1977)? We do not believe the mere existence of a "fixer" invalidates the utility of effective environmental policy studies. Such studies undoubtedly make a fixer's job easier or harder, depending on the overlap between the fixer's intentions and the conclusions of the policy study. Moreover, there is no reason to impute a malevolent motive to a fixer. The reality is that the future holds uncertainties that impact the implementation and ultimate effectiveness of environmental policy. The fixer may have a vital role to play in the implementation of many environmental policies, but effective environmental policy studies are still an important factor that the fixer will have to deal with during implementation.

Why conduct rational analyses of subjective issues that cannot be answered by positive analysis? The argument against rational analysis (and policy studies in general) hinges on the belief that rational analysis cannot alter policy or beliefs. However, rational analysis can influence beliefs if done well. Our review is not comparative; thus our ability to compare the impact of effective versus ineffective policy studies on environmental policy making is limited. We can, however, look at the six studies presented here and conclude that effective environmental policy studies tend to influence subsequent national policy-making efforts when they are used in certain ways.

CONCLUDING REMARKS

We have examined six environmental policy studies in detail. The six case studies we have selected and analyzed are particularly noteworthy because of the impact they have had on actual decision making. Of course, the degree of impact varies considerably. As we have seen, some studies produced recommendations that were not adopted for several years, although they did focus debate by sharpening policy choices at a key moment. We have also discussed the six ways in which effective environmental policy studies tend to be used. As our analysis suggests, effective studies can be used to

- define the problem in a helpful fashion,
- describe the full range of policy options,
- help to overcome agency resistance to change,
- provide opportunities to engage stakeholders,
- enhance the legitimacy of particular actions, and
- help set resource priorities.

Arguably, the more of these functions that a policy study fulfills, the more effective it will be and the greater impact it will have. In Chapter 4, the discussion shifts to how such studies should be organized to maximize their effectiveness.

4

How Policy Studies
Should Be Organized

In Chapter 3 we looked primarily at the way effective environmental policy studies influenced policy. In this chapter we address some of the organizational issues involved in mounting effective environmental policy studies.

SIX ORGANIZATIONAL TASKS

Each time an agency or a legislative committee decides to initiate a study, it must decide what to study and how the research and analysis should be conducted. These decisions cover every facet of the study design and involve six organizational tasks: (1) selecting and using experts (researchers, analysts, and "doers"); (2) shaping the relationship between sponsors and experts; (3) choosing the right institutional auspices; (4) reviewing policy study results using a peer-review process to build technical credibility (incidentally, the study authors must carefully specify the form that recommendations should take in order to ensure that technological advances and improved understandings of hazards and risks will be absorbed; these choices shape the content of the study, its reception by policy makers and the public, and its ultimate impact on policy); (5) learning from policy studies—individuals and organizations should use the study process itself as a learning tool and possibly as an aid; and (6) setting the policy research agenda.

Selecting and Using Experts

Expertise can reside within the organization sponsoring or conducting a study, or it can be brought in from outside. In selecting experts, the study sponsor must first identify the most crucial scientific, technical, economic, social, and political issues involved. Experts should have credibility in these areas. In particular, when policy studies involve significant technical complexity, the experts identified should have in-depth knowledge of the relevant fields. In the cases presented earlier, scientists, engineers, and policy analysts with recognized expertise were engaged from the National Academy of Sciences, Office of Technology Assessment, and the Science Advisory Board of the Environmental Protection Agency (EPA).

In selecting among technical experts, preference should be given to those who are genuinely disinterested (i.e., experts who do not stand to gain or lose personally from a study). This is necessary for the panel to have credibility with the many competing interests involved. Technical and analytical skills alone are insufficient; for an expert to be fully effective, highly developed communication skills, group facilitation skills, and political sensitivity are also essential. Conducting policy studies is both an art and a science, and integrating technical knowledge with social, economic, and political considerations is a unique skill that not all experts possess.

Once experts are identified, they can participate in a number of ways. They can give testimony at hearings, orchestrate data collection and analysis, construct empirical models, oversee the conduct of a study team, advise on implementation, and participate in peer review. Their participation is critical for several reasons. First, the use of experts often enhances the credibility of policy studies in the eyes of policy makers and the public, easing the way for the adoption of legislative reforms, regulations, or other measures. Second, experts from a range of backgrounds can help to ensure that a problem is viewed from numerous perspectives. Third, experts can expedite a study by drawing on past experience and the lessons of parallel research efforts. Finally, experts can help create a persuasive justification for moving forward with new policies, by presenting independent (as opposed to self-serving) arguments for reform. This may be especially important when recommendations are highly political, or likely to be viewed with suspicion by opponents.

In sum, experts in environmental policy studies can

- enhance credibility,
- bring a range of backgrounds to the policy problem,
- draw on parallel research efforts,
- justify moving forward with proposed actions, and
- provide peer review and advice.

CREDIBILITY

The *Delaney Paradox* called upon the expertise of the Board on Agriculture of the National Research Council (NRC) of the National Academy of Sciences (NAS). The Board set up a committee that included experts in pest control, public health, food science, law, and regulatory policy. Because organizations such as the NAS have high standards, their participation in the Delaney study lent significant authority and respect.

However, there are some disadvantages to having such a board undertake a policy study. Jack Moore notes the downside to the NAS approach: "It is very expensive and the NAS delivers on their own time schedule, not yours" (Moore interview, January 3, 1993). Richard Wiles also points out that the *Delaney Paradox* was a "big stretch" for the NAS because, unlike other studies, it is short on science and long on policy. It was not clear whether the NAS would undertake additional policy efforts (Wiles interview, January 26, 1993).

Overall, however, most observers agree that EPA made the right decision in commissioning the Board to undertake the study. As a group of nonpartisan scientists, the Board had the credibility to present controversial findings and withstand the wrath of affected industry groups. Representative Pat Roberts (R-Kansas) reflects on the importance of this choice: "If an 'ag' group does the research, it is just viewed as the fox in the chicken coop." He believes the Board is viewed as "quasi-governmental and independent" and explains, "If you're going to come down from the mountain with a tablet, it's nice to have the NAS name on it" (Foreman & Harsch, 1989).

RANGE OF BACKGROUNDS

Experts from a range of backgrounds can ensure that the problem is viewed from numerous perspectives. Expertise is by nature specific and in-depth. Different fields of study employ different methodologies and emphasize different relations and concepts. Bringing experts together from different fields allows for greater questioning of assumptions and for increased creativity in the study's approach.

For the *Spotted Owl* study, Congress selected four government and academic scientists (the "Gang of Four") who had an intimate knowledge of forest ecosystems. They, in turn, consulted with one hundred experts from a range of disciplines. Expertise was needed both to establish credibility and to provide a body of accurate information within a very tight time frame. John Gordon, one of the four scientists, argues, "Different constituencies with different value systems need a fact base from external sources. Scientific analysis should come in before an issue is too pointed—in this case, it didn't happen until almost too late" (Gordon, personal communication, March 23, 1993).

PARALLEL RESEARCH EFFORTS

Experts can expedite a study by drawing on past experience and the lessons of parallel research. Organizations and bureaucracies are very resistant to change. Often, the lessons of experience within an organization can disappear as personnel change and knowledge shifts. Experts in a particular field keep better track of what has and has not worked than do agency personnel. Competition between experts in a field requires them to keep up with the current state of research. Experts have often conducted research on questions that are similar (if not identical) to the question addressed by the policy study.

In the *Spotted Owl* study, the Gang of Four's task was not to "do science" (i.e., to undertake new experiments), but rather to review existing scientific evidence and make a series of judgments about the likely results of different policies. Gordon describes this process as "science-based assessment" and defines it as "answering a question from outside science based on a synthesis of scientific information" (Gordon, 1993).

MOVING FORWARD WITH PROPOSED ACTIONS

Experts can create a persuasive justification for moving forward. This persuasiveness stems from the continuity of specific, detailed knowledge among professionals in a field. In the *Reducing Risk* study, outside experts were used to strengthen a consensus already emerging in the EPA. The study was conducted by EPA's Science Advisory Board (SAB), a standing panel of academic and professional experts in a variety of scientific and technical disciplines relating to environmental problems (Alm, 1991). The Board also formed a special committee, which consisted of thirty-nine scientists, engineers, and managers with expertise in environment and health problems. The committee was divided into three subcommittees: Ecology and Welfare, Human Health, and Strategic Options. Twelve public meetings were held. Each subcommittee issued a report, which was then included in the main report as an appendix.

None of the ideas in the final report was entirely new. The role of experts was more to synthesize and articulate an already emerging consensus within the agency on the need to redirect EPA's environmental policy to reflect new analytical and policy processes. The breadth and depth of the expertise that contributed to the study lent considerable weight to EPA's call for reshaping priorities. One commentator on the report writes: "The SAB report does not reveal any blinding new insights or divine revelations. . . . It is nevertheless a very influential document. Never before has such a distinguished group of scientists reached such a strong consensus on the need for new directions" (Alm, 1991).

PEER REVIEW AND ADVICE

Sometimes experts are not consulted during the production of an environmental policy study. In these cases, experts can be consulted to review the results after the policy study is written. Outside experts were not used in the *Lead in Gasoline* study, but when it was finished, it was secretly subjected to intensive peer review. The peer review allowed the analysts to broaden their understanding of their own research, refine their work, and address knowledge gaps prior to public evaluation. Leggett reports, "We went through a peer review process which was probably not all that common in that period. We looked for people who stood on all sides of the issue and asked them to provide peer review in secrecy. We got comments back and we incorporated them" (Leggett interview, January 28, 1993).

Expertise plays a large role even when agencies conduct policy studies in-house. Experts are used in these cases either in the review process for the study or in an advisory capacity to guide the work within the agency. In the case of the *Complex Cleanup* study, Congress turned to the Office of Technology Assessment (OTA) for expert advice. Until 1996 the OTA acted as an analytical resource for members of Congress. The OTA's creation in 1972 came out of the growth of the environmental movement, as citizens began to question the technical basis of various federal policies. While OTA analysts accomplished most of the actual work for each study, an advisory committee made up of experts and stakeholders guided the formation of study questions and reviewed analytical methods.

Shaping the Relationship Between Sponsors and Experts

The relationship between the sponsors of an environmental policy study and the experts (researchers, analysts, and "doers") of a policy study should depend on the nature of the study. Conscious choices about how involved the sponsor should be in the actual production of the policy study must be made. Issues that should guide this choice include the level of controversy already existing on the topic, the ultimate purpose of the policy study, the resources available within the sponsoring organization, and the credibility of the sponsoring agency.

There are many different ways to structure a study process. In some instances, the agency or legislative committee sponsoring a study may elect to use an established research organization with a proven track record. Independent bodies typically use time-tested procedures and carry out unbiased analyses. Sponsors may also use a smaller team of behind-the-scenes analysts, including those from within the sponsoring agency itself. The benefits of this approach include the flexibility and the speed that informality permits. Agencies opt for this tactic when they want their staff to be completely familiar with all the technical ins-and-outs of the analyses so they can handle subsequent challenges to the legitimacy of the research. Finally, an advisory board of experts identified by different stakeholder groups can review the work of informal agency teams. This can create an opportunity to involve individuals whose support will be essential to future implementation.

The six cases demonstrate a gradation of possible relationships from sponsor-prepared studies to the use of independent research bodies. The relevant options include:

- Engaging an independent research organization
- Involving stakeholder groups
- Appointing a commission or task force
- Hiring experts directly
- Doing the study in-house

Which institution arrangement will lend the most credibility to the results? There are clearly advantages to sponsoring a formal report prepared by an organization that does not have an immediate stake in the study's outcome. On the other hand, agencies may opt to produce a report internally. Either of these two approaches may include soliciting the advice of stakeholders. Yet a third approach is to invite stakeholders to join in a truly collaborative study design effort. All three approaches can generate influential reports with broad public support.

ENGAGING A MAJOR RESEARCH ORGANIZATION

Probably the most typical way of performing an effective policy study is to get one of the major research organizations such as the OTA, the Congressional Research Service, or the NAS to conduct the study. This approach was used in two of the case studies: *Complex Cleanup* and the *Delaney Paradox*. In both cases, the reputation and independence of these organizations was thought to be necessary for any progress to be made on these issues.

EPA sought out the NAS to perform the *Delaney Paradox* study. Stakeholders were already quite polarized on this issue. Therefore, EPA sought out the most authoritative, independent body it could find. According to Jack Moore, assistant administrator of the EPA for Prevention, Pesticides, and Toxic Substances at the time of the study, "we needed the imprimatur of an NAS committee in order to do something radical in the eyes of some observers" (Moore, 1993). The *Delaney Paradox* was carried out by the Board on Agriculture. The Board selected a seventeen-member committee. Funding was provided by EPA along with some assistance from the Collage Foundation.

The OTA prepared the *Complex Cleanup* study, which used the following methodology:

- Approval of the study methodology and design
- Selection of an advisory committee
- Workshops with experts and stakeholders
- Commissioning consultant research when necessary

The use of OTA to conduct the study was particularly important, especially in light of its most important recommendation for institutional reform of DOE. The Senate Armed Forces Committee, by using OTA to conduct the study, recognized that it is often difficult for any agency to consider and then implement fundamental changes in its management priorities without some external prodding. Moreover, the recognized need for congressional oversight in addition to internal agency reform spurred the Senate Committee's use of OTA.

INVOLVING STAKEHOLDER GROUPS

The *Alternative Agricultural Research and Commercialization (AARC)* study was funded by the USDA. The Task Force on New Farm and Forest Products included a wide circle of outside representatives from the groups most likely to benefit from a national program to promote new products. USDA succeeded in lowering the costs by appointing numerous university and private sector members to the Task Force who were financially supported by their respective institutions. The opportunity thus resulted in a diverse task force representing a broad range of interests.

The Federal Facilities Environmental Restoration Dialogue Committee (FFERDC), which conducted a participatory dialogue over the cleanup of nuclear weapons production facilities, is yet another model for prodding agencies to change. Instead of marshaling state-of-the-art expert opinion from OTA staff, the FFERDC model attempts to push for reform by involving all relevant stakeholders. These stakeholders would collaborate with the Department of Energy (DOE) in conducting the study and would ultimately serve as the watchdogs holding DOE responsible for conducting a "fair" study and ensuring "proper" execution of any resulting recommendations selected for implementation. Whereas the Senate Committee's selection of OTA to conduct the study constituted a "top-down" approach, ultimately requiring DOE compliance subject to congressional oversight, the FFERDC method would have constituted a "bottom-up" approach, holding the DOE accountable to affected stakeholders.

Stakeholder participation may be advisory, as with site specific advisory boards, or it may constitute a true partnership in the ultimate selection of a policy option. Stakeholders can help an agency see shortcomings within its structure and mindset, and thereby may encourage institutional change.

APPOINTING A COMMISSION OR TASK FORCE

Another approach to the relationship between sponsors and experts is for the sponsor to appoint a commission to do the study. Such a commission can be made up of experts with or without stakeholder representatives. This approach is usually used when one of the aims of a policy study is to build a constituency for a new policy direction. This relationship can be seen in both the *Reducing Risk* case study, where EPA turned to its in-house commission of experts, and the *AARC* case, where the USDA put experts and stakeholders together in one body.

The report, *Reducing Risk,* was successful to a much greater degree than the earlier EPA report, *Unfinished Business,* in part because it was not an in-house EPA report. EPA's SAB assembled a study team of outside experts from diverse academic, technical, and policy backgrounds. This was an important strategy because it gave the report credibility both inside and outside the agency, and helped to ensure that the recommendations would be influential in promoting an agenda of a highly political nature: the reshaping of federal environmental objectives.

In the case of AARC, a broad-based task force was created to prod agency action. The diversity of backgrounds among Task Force members allowed in-depth discussion of a variety of policy options. Together they crafted study recommendations covering a wide range of issues that affect new products, from scientific research priorities to industrial development and business financing. Suzette Dittrich believes the study's credibility relied on a multidisciplinary effort with "small business entrepreneurs, large business men and women, educators, scientists, and others" (Dittrich interview, February 29, 1993). Melvin Blase concurs with this assessment and adds that this was "clearly an instance when scientific input into the policy process was important" (Blase, 1993).

HIRING EXPERTS DIRECTLY

There are times when policy studies must be accomplished within time frames that do not allow for the participation of a commission or the methodical work of one of the large research organizations. In the *Spotted Owl* study, Congress hired the scientists directly, a rather unusual approach. Typically, committees seeking expert advice will hold a formal hearing. When they require a formal report on a policy issue, they will usually use one of the many established Washington-based research bodies such as the Congressional Research Service, the OTA, the General Accounting Office (GAO), or the NAS (Lyons & Gordon, 1993). Most of these reports require significant amounts of time for staff to review the subject, interview experts, contract for research, and solicit peer reviews. In this case the two committees agreed that such a lengthy, formal study would not fit the legislative calendar. The hiring of the Gang of Four resulted.

The highly politicized nature of old-growth forest management required that experts be seen as free from bias. Academics and government scientists met this requirement. Although environmental groups were initially suspicious that the government was using its own scientists, they were pleased with the results (Owens personal communication, March 11,

1993). They felt that Congress had embarked on a new approach to policy analysis by asking scientists (not politicians) to develop a policy firmly grounded in ecological principles (Owens, 1993). Moreover, because these scientists were not among the regular group that testified on behalf of environmental groups, and were in some cases directly affiliated with government agencies, it was not easy for the timber industry to dismiss their recommendations as biased.

In part because of their credibility as experts, the Gang of Four was able to help restructure the old-growth forest debate. Following the release of the report, "the debate was no longer over trees and acres, but what risk to species do we want to manage for. It gave the politicians some cover: they could say 'based on the best science, I think this is what we should go for.' The debate continues to be affected by the recognition of the importance of ecosystem science" (Owens, 1993).

DOING THE STUDY IN-HOUSE

In order to do a successful policy study "in-house," the sponsor must make adequate resources available, as the EPA did for the *Lead in Gasoline* case. The EPA believed that it was very important that the study be conducted internally. This was necessary because of the volatile and secret nature of the lead issue. Also, implementation of the study recommendations required that EPA staff know the issue inside and out.

By limiting involvement to a small number of people, EPA made sure that the agency would be ready for implementation. The study was conducted by a small team and was approached as an integrated task. Leggett cites the size of the group as "key" and says that too often policy studies are done by dozens of analysts who rarely talk with one another, each person working on a small piece of the study, which is ultimately glued together with other individual pieces at the end of the effort. From beginning to end, the lead study was an integrated project in the hands of no more than six analysts.

Schwartz adds, "We started out with [a] back of the envelope calculation and then we started going in and taking pieces and making them more complicated and less approximate. A big problem with a lot of analyses is that there are different pieces of it, they get done by different people, they get done sequentially, and after you start doing the second one you realize that the first one wasn't done in the way that was needed for the next part. The key for us was always having an integrated system and making incremental improvements without taking it apart or doing things separately.

We always had a spreadsheet which had the final numbers in it for each of the different categories. Then we could refine a category—it was kind of like replaceable units. . . . It's not like we built 15 different things and at the last step stuck them together—they were always stuck together" (Schwartz interview, January 29, 1993).

The EPA policy analysts were told that the agency was very interested in their work. Too often, government agencies do not view policy analysis as a critical task, and they directly or indirectly transmit this disinterest to their staffs. Joel Schwartz believes the agency's support of the lead study was crucial. He says, "The person running the agency believed in policy analysis. Since (Alm) had a policy orientation, he thought that was a question that the policy office, not the air office, should be asked" (Schwartz, 1993). Jane Leggett concurs: "A lot of the research of the policy office—whether it's good or bad—doesn't go anywhere because people on a staff level . . . are unable to convince people at a higher level that they should undertake it." She concludes that many policy efforts fail because the policy staff are frustrated and not willing to put in the kind of effort invested in the lead study. Leggett argues that staff need to feel that "really important results are coming out and that there is a potential for someone to act on it. Otherwise you're just doing studies and those things tend to drag on over long periods of time" (Leggett, 1993).

EPA provided concrete support to the study as well. The analysts were given high-level administrative support and adequate resources to do their work. Jane Leggett stresses this point: "We were working under ideal conditions—knowing that you had high-level support, feeling like you were getting important findings, knowing that someone would be willing to do something with it, and having enough resources to get the job done." She illustrates her point by noting, "I had the first PC [personal computer] in the agency outside of the Office of Research and Development" (Leggett, 1993).

Even though it was an in-house study, each of the analysts on the lead team had different training, which allowed for a multidisciplinary approach to the policy analysis. Leggett reports, "We had four people with very different expertise and ways of looking at issues. We worked very well as a team together. Having those different points of view, and asking questions of each other by reviewing each other's work, we arrived at different conclusions and covered more of the critical questions than we would have if you had a group with similar expertise and perspective" (Leggett, 1993).

Choosing the Right Institutional Auspices

What institutions will lend credibility to the results? There are clearly advantages to sponsoring a formal report prepared by an organization that does not have an immediate stake in the study's outcome. The numerous, seemingly partisan policy studies conducted concerning the continued use of chlorinated organic compounds discussed in Chapter 1 illustrate this point. On the other hand, agencies may opt to produce a report internally. Either of these two approaches may include soliciting the advice of stakeholders. Yet a third approach represented by the FFERDC process involves inviting stakeholders to join in a truly collaborative effort to design solutions. All three approaches can generate influential reports with broad public support.

A variety of institutions participated in the case studies examined. Institutions such as the NAS are well-respected, elite organizations whose publications on science policy are widely read and deemed very credible by policy makers. Similarly, the OTA was created by Congress to research and assess the policy implications of the choices we make about what technologies to use. Until it was dismantled in 1996, it played a valuable role. Environmental policy decisions should be made based upon the best scientific data available. Thus scientists have a role in developing innovative approaches that will assist in the making of new policy decisions. They can also redefine the questions being asked by policy makers and in turn change the terms of the political debate. Science as an institution is both affected by and affects the analysis of environmental policy. The Board on Agriculture, which conducted the *Delaney Paradox* study, is a part of the NAS, a reliable and well-respected research organization.

For the *Spotted Owl* study, scientists were selected from the government and the academic community. Environmentalists were unsure whether the government scientists could produce a study free of policy bias. The highly politicized nature of the old-growth forest issue convinced Congress of the need to find experts who would be seen as free from bias. Both academics and government scientists were able to meet this requirement. Although environmental groups were initially suspicious that the government was using its own scientists, they were pleased with the results (Owens, 1993). Because these scientists did not regularly testify on behalf of environmental groups, and were in some cases directly affiliated with government agencies, it was not easy for the timber industry to dismiss their recommendations as biased.

The *Lead in Gasoline* study was internal. By limiting involvement to a small number of people, EPA made sure that the agency would be ready for implementation. The study was conducted by a small team and approached as an integrated effort. The size of the team and in-house nature of the study were critical factors leading to the success of the study.

The *AARC* study was affiliated and funded by the USDA. The Task Force also included a wide circle of outside representatives from the groups most likely to benefit from a national program to promote new products. Policy studies are often expensive. USDA succeeded in lowering the costs by appointing numerous university and private sector members to the Task Force who were financially supported by their respective institutions. Blase reports that "deans were delighted to pick up the bills," and that the same was true for much of industry (Blase, 1993).

The use of OTA to conduct the *Complex Cleanup* study was particularly important, especially in light of its most important recommendation—institutional reform of DOE. The Senate Armed Forces Committee, by using OTA to conduct the study, recognized that it is often difficult for any agency to consider and then implement fundamental changes in its own management priorities without some external prodding.

The FFERDC process was another results-oriented method. Under the FFERDC method, stakeholders collaborated with DOE in conducting the study and ultimately served as the watchdogs holding DOE responsible for conducting a "fair" study and ensuring "proper" execution of any resulting recommendations selected for implementation. Utilizing institutions such as OTA, and ultimately the FFERDC method, added to the impact of this study.

Reviewing Policy Study Results

Results of a policy study must be critically appraised before they are released. In some of our cases, evaluation was built into the preparation of the study, as agency personnel or stakeholders were invited to review or comment on the findings as the study progressed. In other instances, there was a formal peer review process once the research was completed. In any review process, differing views on the issues involved must be fully explored, and those most likely to be critical should be given an opportunity to preview the results and provide comments. In general, evaluation helps to ensure that the study has considered important policy questions comprehensively and properly, and thereby enhances the credibility of the study.

The *Delaney Paradox* was subject to the NAS guidelines for peer review. (See Appendix A containing the NAS review guidelines.) The *Lead in Gasoline* report was peer reviewed after it was drafted. Due to time concerns, the *Spotted Owl* report was not subjected to formal peer review, but the scientists did consult with a broad range of experts. However, subsequent research has not substantially challenged the Gang of Four's conclusions (Gordon, 1993). The study provides an example of a "successful" policy study that was generated outside of a formal institutional process, and which never received a peer review.

Complex Cleanup was reviewed by an outside panel of experts put together by OTA. While it existed, OTA provided a useful model of formal report making. To maintain its credibility in the field, OTA followed a standard procedure for all reports. This procedure included:

- Selection of an advisory committee representing diverse interests
- Workshops with a range of experts
- Commissioning consultant research when necessary
- Peer review of the draft report

One of the main goals of the *Reducing Risk* study was to review EPA's report entitled *Unfinished Business*. The SAB, which conducted the review, is affiliated with EPA, but it is also a standing committee of outside experts. Therefore, the report was essentially a peer review of the earlier EPA report, which had been strictly an internal document. Although the Board strongly agreed with the basic concept of using comparative risk to structure environmental priorities, it also had many criticisms. One of the criticisms was that EPA staff did not assess environmental problems in areas that had not historically fallen under EPA's jurisdiction, such as agriculture and transportation. This failing is perhaps symptomatic of a more general problem: It is difficult for agencies to produce internal reports that can analyze problems comprehensively and objectively, free from a set of long-standing preconceptions about current institutional arrangements and policy frameworks.

A second issue that must be addressed during the review process is the form that any policy recommendation should take. One of the most important factors contributing to the success of the *AARC* study was its format. The *Task Force* study is easy to read, attractive, and a "quick study" for busy policy makers. Blase stresses the importance of the format: "As silly as it may sound, I think the red cover on the report made it stand out—people knew it by the color." The report has a very short and carefully worded executive summary that is printed separately from the study itself. Blase says this was important "because a person could pick it up and within 15 minutes get the essence of our recommendations" (Blase, 1993).

Since the study will act as a basis for future laws and regulations, the recommendations must take future technological and knowledge changes into account. The *Lead in Gasoline* study sought to modify existing regulatory criteria concerning permissible lead levels in gasoline. An increased understanding of the risks associated with lead greatly helped to implement the study's recommendations.

Dr. Robert M. White, president emeritus of the National Academy of Engineering (NAE), former vice chairman of the NAS's NRC, and author of the NAE book entitled *Keeping Pace with Science and Engineering*, notes that "legislated criteria are generally an amalgam of scientific knowledge and the value judgments of our representatives in the legislature" (White, 1993). Uncertainties in our understanding of hazards, risks, costs, and benefits are high with respect to environmental laws and regulations because such laws usually address issues at the cutting edge of scientific understanding. Thus finding ways to incorporate future advances in technology as well as knowledge of hazards and risks is an issue of paramount importance.

White provides the following examples of legislation that attempts to incorporate future technological advances: "Some national environmental legislation recognizes the dynamic nature of the technical basis for regulation. In some cases, it mandates research and development programs to improve the data base. In other cases, it provides incentives for the development of new, more cost-effective technology. In still other cases, legislation explicitly includes schedules for reconsidering specific regulatory decisions" (White, 1993). However, even with the above provisions in place, it is still a difficult task to modify environmental laws and regulations.

The *Delaney Paradox* recommended changing existing law. The study demonstrates just how difficult it is to incorporate technological advancements into existing legal frameworks. Due to tremendous improvement in the technology for measuring trace substances in food as well as our improved understanding of the risks associated with these trace elements, the EPA felt confident supporting the recommendations contained in the

Delaney Paradox (White, 1993). However, since the original clause did not permit any "modification," the recommendations have proven extremely difficult to implement, requiring nearly a decade to be enacted formally.

Learning from Policy Studies

The ability to use policy studies to catalyze and guide the efforts of federal agencies can be enhanced as individuals and organizations that conduct such studies assimilate the lessons learned from experience. Following are three possible approaches to ensure that the appropriate lessons are not lost.

CROSS-CASE ANALYSIS

Cross-case analysis is essential to identify what works and what does not. Some of the many questions that can be analyzed with other, similar cases include: How did decisions about the use of experts and the participation of stakeholders shape the credibility of the final recommendations? How were the new proposals received by the public and the media? How did the design of the study affect implementation? Were the study's recommendations successful in generating policy change in the federal or state arenas? Individuals not involved in any of the cases should be selected to do cross-case analysis.

The notion of comparative risk has evolved over a series of reports and programmatic efforts varying in scale from EPA pilot projects to agency-wide reviews and independent, external critiques. In addition, state and local agencies have repeated the "comparative risk reduction" process. These state and local studies usually differ from EPA's national study because they employ a more collaborative approach; a broad range of stakeholders, not just experts, tend to be involved. The *Reducing Risk* study reflected this broader participation. The Relative Risk Reduction Strategies Committee (RRRSC), and particularly the Human Health Subcommittee, found it difficult to rank risk without information on public values. They found that ranking risk goes beyond technical issues to include explicit value considerations. Subsequent efforts have attempted to address this concern by bringing in many different sectors of the affected community. Participants in these comparative risk processes learn from each other, and often become advocates for the process (Manard personal communication, March 16, 1993).

The *Spotted Owl* report has provided a successful model for environmental policy studies that can be repeated by different agencies. The approach taken by the scientists encouraged a much broader view of the problem, and one that departed from the normal "problem of the moment" view that often persists on Capitol Hill (Lyons personal communication, February, 1993). The Governor of Georgia has since asked the same four scientists to do a similar study. The House Agriculture and House Merchant Marine Committees are also looking to do analogous studies on northern forests.

The comprehensive "ecosystem management" approach recommended in the *Spotted Owl* report seems to have become a model for resource management. In 1993, the House Natural Resources Committee was still seeking ecosystem management models that could be used across the country (Owens, 1993). The Committee was motivated by the belief that land managers must consider the cumulative impact of activities such as mining and grazing on a variety of species, and on entire watersheds.

DOCUMENTING THE PROCESS OF ANALYSIS IN "REAL TIME"

Decisions and outcomes in each case can only be documented effectively in real time. Documentation enables a research team and sponsors of a study to receive a neutral, critical assessment of the direction and quality of their work right after it is completed. Outside specialists can be brought in to document the study process as it happens (which also will facilitate cross-case analysis after the fact). Such feedback can be used to make substantive or procedural adjustments. These adjustments are more likely to be on target if they are suggested by someone who has followed the study closely.

FINDING OUT WHAT THE RESULTS ARE

Organizations that conduct or sponsor studies should draft follow-up procedural guidelines that incorporate or institutionalize what they have learned. Guidelines can translate the lessons learned from earlier experiences into tangible steps that can help subsequent researchers and sponsors. As they are applied and tested in practice, written guidelines gradually become norms familiar to and recognized by all staff members in an organization. The preparation of written guidelines will also enhance the credibility of a study by ensuring stakeholders (particularly sponsors) that the research underpinning policy recommendations was carried out using "time-tested" procedures.

Setting the Policy Research Agenda

Some may think that a discussion of how to decide what policy issues to study should have come earlier in this book. In many ways, though, selecting what to study is an outgrowth of acquired policy experience and thus follows our discussion of how to learn from policy studies.

Often individuals think they know what to study because they are knowledgeable about a topic. More basic questions, however, are even more important. One way of focusing a study effort is known as "futures research." This is particularly relevant when considering environmental issues. As our discussion of the possible regulation of chlorinated organic compounds in Chapter 1 indicated, many environmental issues involve substantial scientific uncertainty.

Futures research, forecasting, and a host of other terms describe techniques for predicting future events, trends, and issues even in the face of enormous uncertainty. Or, as Theodore Gordon describes it, "Futures research is the systematic exploration of what might be" (1992). There are many futures research techniques employed by forecasters. Table 4-1 identifies a selection of them.

Qualitative	Quantitative	Indirect
Intuition	Naive Methods	Market Surveys
Expert Opinion	Moving Averages	Input/Output Analysis
Delphi Technique	Exponential Smoothing	Economic Indicators
Scenarios	Trend Analysis	
Assumptions	Decomposition of Time Series	
PERT - Derived	Box-Jenkins	
Simulation	Simple Regression	
Cross-Impact Analysis	Multiple Regression	
Expert Systems	Econometric Modeling	
Scanning		

Table 4-1. Forcasting Methods.

Certain futures research techniques are more appropriate for business forecasting, others for macroeconomic forecasting, and still others for technology forecasting. No matter which technique is ultimately selected, certain "axioms" should be kept in mind:

- Forecasting techniques generally assume that the same underlying causal relationship that existed in the past will continue to prevail in the future—in other words, extrapolation is bound to be wrong eventually.
- Forecasts are seldom perfect.
- Forecast accuracy decreases as the range of the forecast increases.
- Forecasts for groups of items tend to be more accurate than forecasts for individual items (Shim, Siegel, & Liew, 1994).

In addition, Gordon (1992) adds:

- Forecasts can be very precise but quite inaccurate.
- Forecasts are incomplete—"The most surprising future is one in which there are no surprises."
- Forecasts can be self-fulfilling or self-defeating.

Futures research has been used in environmental policy making. Indeed, future thinking, principally by environmental policy experts like Lynton K. Caldwell, was the prime factor in the eventual passage of the National Environmental Policy Act (NEPA) in 1970. Since its inception, EPA has targeted prevailing environmental problems. However, the increasing rate of change, primarily in the field of technology, has effectively shrunk the distance between the present and the future. These changes threaten to render present EPA approaches ineffectual in dealing with future environmental problems (Loehr, 1995). The EPA has utilized futures research techniques to chart new directions for the agency for the coming millennium. In 1993, the EPA charged its SAB to

- assess different methodologies currently being used to study possible futures and anticipate likely futures events,
- identify some environmental issues that could emerge over the long term (through the year 2025), and
- advise EPA on ways to incorporate futures research into the Agency's activities (U.S. Environmental Protection Agency, 1995).

The SAB formed the Futures Research Committee to address this assignment. In January 1995, after a year and a half, the Committee published its findings in a report entitled *Beyond the Horizon: Using Foresight to Protect the Environmental Future.*

The Environmental Futures Committee, after examining and evaluating the applicability of various futures research techniques, identified three promising approaches: (1) scenarios—or top-down approach, (2) look-out panel—or bottom-up approach, and (3) scanning. Although the Committee considered each method, it did not compare them in detail. Likewise, the Committee declined to state a preference for one technique.

The Committee suggested that as an essential part of its future capabilities, EPA should establish an early-warning system to identify potential future environmental risks. This early warning system should rely on scenarios, a look-out panel, and scanning as input sources. The Committee also recommended that in the longer-term, EPA should focus on five overarching problems:

- Sustainability of terrestrial ecosystems
- Noncancer human health effects
- Total air pollutant loadings
- Nontraditional environmental stressors
- Health of the oceans

Finally, the Committee stressed that EPA, as well as other agencies and organizations, should recognize that global environmental quality is a matter of strategic national interest (Environmental Futures Committee, 1995). Thus, futures research can play a variety of roles in environmental policy studies. First, futures research can help to set the agenda. Second, it offers a way of tracking important structural changes. Third, futures research can help promote better integration of planning and implementation processes (Amara, 1991).

A LOOK IN THE REARVIEW MIRROR

One area not yet discussed relates to the validity of the underlying data, statistics, and other facts gathered for a study. Any inaccuracy or fault in the data, statistics, or facts may skew the results, resulting in erroneous policy recommendations. If policy makers subsequently rely on the recommendations of the study, the results can be disastrous. Such an event would not only erode the credibility of the sponsors, experts, and others involved, but could very well be deleterious to human health and the environment. According to Dr. Robert M. White, president emeritus of the NAE and former vice chairman of the NRC, "When environmental regulatory costs turn out in retrospect to have been unwarranted because regulatory decisions were based on inadequate or inaccurate scientific information, it's only natural to express concern, since costs will have been borne without deriving the projected environmental benefits" (White, 1993).

Factual error can occur in three ways. First, the actual data collected may be improperly recorded. Likewise, a latent error may be present in the statistical data collected. A second type of error can occur when the factual data were themselves accurate but the experts involved interpreted them incorrectly. Dr. White warns that "in environmental . . . affairs, we frequently are confronted with data for which neither the level of precision nor the level of accuracy is particularly high" (White, 1993). Finally, a third type of error occurs when the factual data are accurate, but the wrong data were utilized in the policy study. This third type of error occurs when data on the wrong parameters are used in the study or when data concerning all of the relevant parameters are not used (Eberstadt, 1995). Closely related to this third type of error is the situation that occurs when the data are accurate by today's technological standards, but may become obsolete with future improvements in data collection.

In many cases it is extremely difficult to identify these errors because they often manifest themselves long after the implemented aims of the policy study recommendations fail to achieve the desired results. However, several steps can be taken to help reduce the incidence of these kinds of errors. Errors in faulty data can be eliminated or at least identified by the experts doing the study. Questionable data may require testing or re-collection to provide the proper baseline data necessary. The first type of error can sometimes be identified and corrected during the peer review process.

The second type of error, erroneous application of accurate data, is more difficult to identify, but can also be detected during the peer review process. "While there may be differences among the parties in their attitudes about what constitutes proper review and evaluation, no one argues that the data ought not to be subject [to rigorous peer review], which presumably results in a body of technical evidence that represents the best that is available at a given time" (White, 1993).

The third type of error, utilizing accurate but inappropriate data, or not considering all the potential parameters, is the most difficult to rectify. A recent study of recycling policies in Pittsburgh, Pennsylvania, unearthed some previously overlooked weaknesses. The study determined that existing recycling policies in Pittsburgh were not economically sound, due in part to the fluctuating market for recyclable materials. Moreover, recycling was not environmentally sound because the negative environmental impacts from the recyclable materials collection process far outweighed the benefits, especially given existing landfill policy and improvements in landfill technology. The Pittsburgh study implies that environmental policy studies need to look at all of the dimensions of a problem and how the parameters interrelate amongst themselves (Hendrickson, Lave, & McMichael, 1995).

A second example of this third type of error was the "mercury in fish" scare. The cause of high mercury in fish was believed to be due to industry discharging heavy metals into the oceans. The scare resulted in a prohibition on the harvest of fish above a certain weight. However, after an examination of museum specimens, researchers discovered that, except in certain isolated incidents, the mercury in ocean fish reflected naturally occurring levels of mercury in the oceans (White, 1993). In this case, early examination of all of the relevant parameters might have anticipated an expensive, but inappropriate reaction.

The problems caused by this third type of error are not insurmountable. Several of the case studies utilized techniques to forestall this third type of error. The *Lead in Gasoline* study looked at a large number of potential effects caused by existing lead levels in gasoline. Although existing lead levels in gasoline had a number of environmental impacts, the study was able to link lead levels in gasoline with the incidence of high blood pressure in human beings. Had the study experts not explored this particular impact on humans, it is quite possible the study would not have resulted in lowering lead levels in gasoline. The study also had a much broader impact in light of more recent determinations indicating that the risks associated with exposure to lead were greater than previously thought (White, 1993).

In the *Spotted Owl* study, the Gang of Four set out to study the differing effects of policy recommendations not only on one species, the spotted owl, but on all of the species in the relevant ecosystem likely to be affected by proposed policy changes. The Gang of Four recognized that a particular policy choice, though beneficial to both industry and the spotted owl, might have unanticipated consequences on other species in the ecosystem. As previously mentioned the Gang of Four consulted experts from over one hundred different fields to make sure they considered all of the relevant factors likely to have an impact on the spotted owl.

CONCLUDING REMARKS

Organizing effective policy studies may appear at the outset to be a daunting task. Although differing approaches can be taken by the many organizations that conduct policy studies, the following organizational tasks can make the difference between an effective and an ineffective policy study:

- Selecting and using experts (researchers, analysts, "doers")
- Shaping the relationship between sponsors and experts
- Choosing the right institutional auspices
- Reviewing policy study results
- Learning from the study
- Setting the policy research agenda

There is a need for precise and accurate data collection when conducting environmental policy studies. Inaccurate data can have devastating consequences for the environment and human health. By looking at data from other areas that relate to the issue at hand, new insights may be achieved as to the most important parameters to be addressed in a policy study.

As the cases demonstrate, there is no single approach that will ensure an effective policy study. Each environmental problem must be addressed in a situationally appropriate way. Issue volatility, political pressure, risk analysis, institutional constraints, and the scientific and technical issues involved are just some of the factors that must be taken into account when organizing a policy study. Using the cases in this volume as a guide should prove beneficial in assessing the factors likely to have an impact in a given policy study.

5

Methods and Roles of Environmental Policy Studies

In 1951, Harold Lasswell noted that the term *policy science* meant "applied social and psychological science." The term *policy analyst* meant "political scientist." The term *policy* itself was "commonly used to designate the most important choices made either in organized or private life" (Lasswell, 1951). These definitions are still critical to our understanding of policy science.

The beginnings of policy science can be traced to the time of World War I, when the social, psychological, and other applied sciences contributed greatly to the conduct of war. Economists estimated the resources, manpower, and facilities required. Psychologists developed intelligence tests as a means of selecting individuals to perform particular tasks. The economists relied on mathematics and statistics while the psychologists used other quantitative methods. The emphasis on such methods reflected the view of many social scientists that they would gain greater acceptance the more closely their "tools" approximated those of the physical sciences. In the early 1920s, Charles E. Merriman, professor of political science at the University of Chicago, formed the Social Science Research Council, a group of scholars in political science, economics, sociology, and psychology, which stressed the importance of breaking down the barriers between scholars and enhancing the study of methods. In the preface to his book, *New Aspects of Politics*, Merriman sought "to suggest certain possibilities of approach to method, in the hope that others may take up the task and through reflection and experiment eventually introduce more intelligent and scientific technique into the study and practice of government, and into popular attitudes toward the governing process" (Lasswell, 1951). Many similar groups formed during the period between the two wars.

Improvements in social science research methods resulted in increasing capacity to make primary observations and process data. During the period of the depression in the United States, policy science came into its own with the realization that government intervention was essential in order to address the issue of unemployment and to set in motion the forces of the free market. Until that time, "economic theory" had cautioned against drastic government action. World War II witnessed an increasing and more effective use of the skills of economists, psychologists, sociologists, and social psychologists (Lasswell, 1951). Although the groundwork for policy science was laid, the parameters of policy science had not yet been set.

The introduction and subsequent development of applied social science methods inevitably led to the question of how this new knowledge should be used. Lasswell stated that the resources of the expanding fields of social science should "be directed toward the basic conflicts in our civilization . . . by the application of scientific method to the study of personality and culture" (1951). He further noted the importance of selecting fundamental problems, the use of models, the clarification of goals, the need to maintain a global perspective, and the value of building institutions to foster the association between active policy makers and academicians (Lasswell, 1951).

Lasswell underscored the desirability of integrating "the intellectual life" and harmonizing science and practice. A "policy orientation," he argued, required an emphasis on process and on the intelligence needs of policy. Or, to put it another way, policy science includes: "(1) the methods by which the policy process is investigated; (2) the results of the study of policy; and (3) the findings of the disciplines making the most important contributions to the intelligence needs of the time" (Lasswell, 1951). Ultimately, this view of a "policy orientation" emerged as what we know as policy analysis.

APPROACHES TO POLICY STUDIES

Since Lasswell's early writings on policy science, the field has continued to evolve. Quade and Carter (1989) define policy analysis as "attempting to bring modern science and technology to bear on society's problems . . . [by] search[ing] for feasible courses of action, generating information and marshaling evidence of the benefits and other consequences that would follow their adoption and implementation, in order to help the policy maker choose the most advantageous action." Operations research, systems analysis, and cost–benefit analysis are some of the methods often used to conduct policy analyses. However, the term *policy analysis* has a broader connotation than the analysis itself and generally encompasses the political and organizational difficulties associated with making policy decisions and then implementing them (Quade & Carter, 1989).

In general, the techniques of policy analysis emphasize a structured and systematic approach characterized by the need to: (1) define a problem and develop evaluative criteria; (2) generate policy options, forecast future requirements, and predict consequences; and (3) evaluate and rank alternative policy options (Carley, 1980).

Systems Analysis

In a narrow sense, systems analysis characterizes one approach used in policy analysis. In its broadest sense it can actually substitute for the broad definition of policy analysis offered above. To fully comprehend the scope of systems analysis, operations research must first be briefly examined.

Operations research (OR) is a tool that helps management determine its policies and actions scientifically. Stated in a more pragmatic way, it is the use of "scientific methods to help decision makers get the most out of available resources" by manipulating them more effectively (Quade & Carter, 1989). OR traces its origins to World War II, when it was first employed in the defense arena to handle complex problems involving large systems composed of men, machines, and other resources. Today it is used widely in business and industrial arenas (Quade & Carter, 1989).

Utilizing OR, analysts develop a simplified mathematical model of a complex system and then add estimates of risk and chance in an attempt to predict and compare the outcomes of several alternative decisions or strategies. Unlike some areas of science, where the models are often based on a well-understood and confirmed body of scientific knowledge, the OR analyst is frequently challenged by "systems" for which no established theory exists. To construct a model, the OR analyst organizes numerical inputs based on intuition (and limited practical experience). As experience with the relevant system increases or when data from experimentation become available, the analyst modifies or even completely discards earlier models (Quade & Carter, 1989).

OR is best at addressing "efficiency problems." Systems analysis more generally applies to the task of making an "optimal choice." Where OR was frequently used to address relatively simple problems where the decision makers had clear objectives in mind, systems analysis was applied to more complex problems involving unclear policy objectives. Systems analysis is thus often employed for the selection of an appropriate mix of goals and frequently takes forecasts of future economic factors into account (Quade & Carter, 1989).

Systems analysis thus takes OR one step further; it not only collects and analyzes quantitative data, it also addresses the question of what then to do with them. Quade and Carter (1989) describe the process of systems analysis as including: (1) objectives, (2) alternatives, (3) impacts, (4) criteria, and (5) models.

Objectives specify what the decision maker hopes to achieve. Frequently, objectives will not be clearly stated and the analyst will have to investigate and broker agreement on policy objectives. Where there is more than one decision maker (as in a legislative body), the analyst may have to infer objectives from written documents or published statements. Once objectives are established, the analyst must then identify alternatives by which the objectives can be achieved.

The alternatives considered are not necessarily obvious substitutes for each other, nor do they necessarily involve the same specific functions. Some alternatives may only emerge after a first round of analysis is conducted, posing new alternatives to consider. After identifying alternatives, the analyst must then address the likely consequences of each.

Impacts are often cast as costs (negative factors) and benefits (positive factors). Costs and benefits may sometimes overlap (as when a cost to one decision maker may be a benefit to another). When addressing impacts, the analyst must also consider distant consequences, which may not directly affect the attainment of the objectives but may be of particular concern to a key decision maker.

Criteria are rules or standards the analyst uses to rank alternatives in terms of how well they achieve the objectives. Thus, criteria connect objectives, alternatives, and impacts.

Models are at the heart of systems analysis. Models are used to predict the consequences of a particular alternative. When building a model, the analyst must test for consistency the logic of assumptions about operations, and use data from the world-at-large to evaluate the strength of hypothesized relationships. In this manner, model-building can enhance understanding of a situation even before the consequences of particular alternatives are evaluated using the model (Quade & Carter, 1989).

The five elements of a systems analysis described above are woven together to form an analytic process with five phases (Quade & Carter, 1989):

1. *Formulation*—clarifying and constraining the problem and determining the objectives
2. *Search*—identifying, designing, and screening alternatives
3. *Forecasting*—predicting the future environment or operational context
4. *Modeling*—building and using models to determine impacts
5. *Synthesis*—comparing and ranking alternatives

Often, this process needs to be performed several times before a "best" alternative can be identified.

Figure 5-1 illustrates how the systems analysis methodology outlined above fits into public policy analysis more generally.

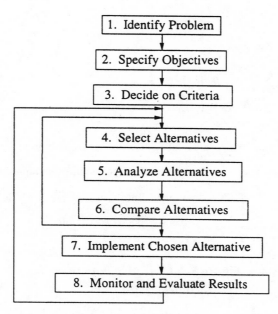

Figure 5-1. Steps in a Public Policy Analysis.
(Walker & Fisher, 1994).

Steps 2 through 6 clearly involve systems analysis. Public policy analysis must include problem identification and objective setting (steps 1 and 2) as well as implementation (step 7) and monitoring and evaluation (step 8). The feedback loops illustrate the iterative nature of the process. In addition, these feedback loops indicate that as the process progresses, analysts, their sponsors, and those likely to be affected learn from previous work. Decision makers for whom the work is being done are also influenced by pressure from interested constituents, and from still other decision makers who may see their domain adversely affected by what they anticipate as the likely impact of certain policy alternatives. Hence objectives and alternatives change, and constraints are introduced and removed. This is one of the major reasons why systems analysis must be a repetitive process (Findeisen & Quade, 1985).

Many models have been developed to compare and rank alternatives (step 6). Often the relative merits of alternatives are described in terms of one, or at most a few, indicators (index value, figure of merit, or objective function). For example, an objective function is a type of linear program (LP) model that seeks to maximize a limited set of objectives, or Z function. The objective function may be stated as shown in Figure 5-2.

Minimize: $Z = \sum_{j=1}^{n} c_j x_j$

Subject to: $\sum_{j=1}^{n} a_{i,j} x_j \geq b_i$, for $i=1,...,m$

$x_j \geq 0$ for $j=1,...,n$

Where: $x_1, x_2, ... , x_n$ are nonnegative decision variables or unknowns; and

$c_1, c_2, ... , c_n$ are contribution coefficients that represent the

marginal contribution to Z for each unit of their

respective decision variable.

Figure 5-2. Objective Function.
(Schniederjans, 1995).

The objective function is subject to a set of m constraints. Each constraint that makes up an LP model is a separate function, called a functional. These functionals may be viewed as individual objectives or goals to be attained. In effect, the b_i are a set of objectives or goals that must be satisfied in order for a solution to be feasible. Also, optimization of the objective function is secondary to finding a feasible solution set of the x_j that will satisfy all of the constraints in a model. In addition, LP models are implicitly based on several other assumptions, including the certainty assumption: all parameters, a_{ij}, b_i, and c_j must be known with certainty (Schniederjans, 1995).

Decision Theory

Decision theory developed as an approach to working with uncertainties in the context of an analysis. Specifically, decision theory involves the selection of an optimal alternative based upon contingent probabilities— likelihoods that events will occur and will influence the benefits or the costs associated with various policy alternatives (Raiffa, 1968; Nagel, 1984). In the same way that systems analysis represented a leap forward as compared with operations research, so too does decision theory, even though future factors may be extremely difficult to predict with accuracy. In these situations, there are a number of approaches that can be used:

- *Delay*—defer the analysis until more or better information is available.
- *Purchase Information*—fund additional research or data collection.
- *Hedge*—consider alternative options or modify alternatives to give greater flexibility.
- *Compromise*—select an alternative that is not optimal given the most likely contingency, but that is not too bad considering alternative contingencies.
- *Be Conservative*—adopt a "max–min" alternative that represents the best alternative assuming the worst contingency occurs.

Decision theory argues that the probabilities of these future factors are not entirely unknown nor beyond human judgment. It calls for the analyst to assign probabilities "objectively" (Schwartz et al., 1985). After assigning probabilities, the analyst must then select appropriate evaluation criteria to evaluate the alternatives (e.g., cost–benefit analysis of expected values).

The principal advantage of decision theory rests with the fact that it permits the consideration of compromise actions (alternatives) that are neither absolutely optimal nor efficient. Moreover, because of its statistical underpinnings, decision theory accommodates formulations involving repeated designs of models or experiments (Raiffa, 1968).

Institutional Rational Choice Theory

Institutional rational choice theory is a complex concept that rests on the idea that the institutional context of a decision maker is a critical element in setting objectives and in recommending or selecting particular policy options. Rational choice theory is not a method of policy analysis but a theory for selecting and recommending policy alternatives which themselves are a result of a policy analysis.

In a simple model of choice, if alternative A_1 results in outcome O_1 while alternative A_2 results in outcome O_2, and O_1 is more desirable than O_2, rational choice theory dictates that A_1 should be chosen over A_2. The selection of a policy alternative is thus value laden—requiring the determination of which outcome is more valuable and why. However, the simple rational choice model only works when there is a single decision maker, the outcome can be predicted with certainty, and the resulting consequences are immediate (because the value of the outcome will change over time) (Dunn, 1994).

When there are many decision makers, as in a legislative body, individual legislators exercise their own values in selecting a policy alternative. When alternatives can be consistently ranked—based on one or more attributes—the situation is referred to in rational choice theory as being transitive. However, when there are many decision makers with differing or conflicting objectives, the situation is called intransitive. The intransitive situation requires moving beyond the simple choice model to what is called the complex choice model. Just because a situation is intransitive does not mean that a rational choice cannot be made. In a complex, intransitive situation there are a number of rational grounds for supporting a particular policy:

- *Technical rationality*—reasoned choices that compare alternatives with respect to their ability to promote effective solutions
- *Economic rationality*—reasoned choices that compare alternatives with respect to their efficient solutions

- *Legal rationality*—reasoned choices that compare alternatives based on their conformity to established rules and precedents
- *Social rationality*—reasoned choices that compare alternatives based on their ability to maintain or improve social institutions
- *Substantive rationality*—reasoned choices that compare alternatives based on all of these forms of situational rationality (Dunn, 1994).

Often, policy alternatives can be justified on a multirational basis. Rational choice theory attempts to explain how and why policy options are ultimately selected.

Institutional rational choice theory takes this process one step further by recognizing that decision makers operate within their institutional contexts, which in turn affect the choices made. The role of institutions is presented by Vickers as twofold: Institutions or organizations are entities that can be studied themselves; individual decision makers play institutional roles (1995). Vickers further distinguishes the choices a decision maker must make in the context of market choice (i.e., an individual chooses for himself) or political choice (i.e., an individual chooses for many).

Kiser and Ostrom (1982) describe five factors that help to explain an individual's behavior within an institutional structure:

- The decision maker
- The community affected by independent decision making
- Events
- Institutional arrangements
- The decision situation in which individuals make choices

By focusing on each element above, public policy theorists attempt to explain actions in terms of both individual decision makers and aggregated decisions. In this sense, institutional rational decision theory examines not only the individual values that a rational decision maker relies on to select among policy alternatives, but also incorporates the reality of institutional forces that shape the process of selection.

Policy Analysis Within the Political Context

The previous sections of this chapter have documented the rise of policy science and examined various approaches to policy analyses. In this section we delve further into the political role that policy analysis has played.

Wildavsky (1987) examines policy analysis from the standpoint of advocacy and then explores the importance of problem identification, knowledge, and citizens in the process. He begins by framing policy analysis as a change in patterns of social interaction:

> *Policy analysis, as I conceive it, is about change in patterns of social interaction. How does change happen? By joining planning to politics, social interaction gives analysis a historical outlook made up of the past pattern of agreements, including agreements to disagree until next time. From the organized actors, the constituent elements of this interaction, analysis gets its abiding interest in incentives to alter their behavior. And planning helps analysis bring intelligence to interaction, by rationalizing movement to a different pattern that may lead to improved future outcomes.* (Wildavsky, 1987, p. 139)

Policy analysis is composed of both intelligence and social interaction. If analysis were purely intellectual, analysts would take center stage. Likewise, if policy analysis were totally interactive, there would be no need for analysts. Wildavsky's view of policy analysis is actually a hybrid of intellect and interaction that uses intelligence to help guide social interaction. By defining rationality in policy analysis as being both retrospective (objectives absent in the present are retrospectively rationalized) and prospective (as discussed earlier), Wildavsky argues that planning and politics do not differ with respect to reason.

Wildavsky's view of policy problem identification and definition also represents the evolution of the field. Previously, a set of fundamental policy problems were identified and analyzed within the constraints imposed by the notion in social science theory that individual choice is controlled by thoughts and values that are passively received from the surrounding culture. Wildavsky disagreed with the notion that culture was "a fixed set of logical pigeonholes." Instead, just as "problems are man-made, so is culture." Because life is not merely a matter of producing given values, but an exploration of the field of values itself, creativity then can be thought of as the conceptualization of new problems. Just as scientists view prohibitions (constraints) as challenges to be met, tested, and perhaps invalidated or overcome, policy analysts should view constraints not merely as obstacles but opportunities that challenge the analyst to determine how they can be overcome (Wildavsky, 1987).

In an attempt to characterize the most fundamental interactions between policy analysis and politics and to explore how analytic integrity can be combined with political efficacy, Wildavsky examined the role of knowledge and power within the context of a "self-evaluating organization." Such an ideal organization would be one that continually monitors its own activities so that it can determine not only how well it meets its objectives, but whether the objectives ought to be changed. Unfortunately, such self-evaluating organizations are hard to find. Instead, evaluation remains, if it occurs at all, as a minor element in administrative organizations. Knowledge can play an important role in a self-evaluating administrative organization, particularly in those where the pursuit of evaluative results has an important role to play in policy setting. Without power, knowledge is difficult to obtain. Organizations may have to change their goals as a condition for receiving information. Knowledge can be used to enhance power, which in turn can result in an increased ability to obtain additional knowledge. Wildavsky concludes that organizations must balance the need for knowledge with the exercise of power so that knowledge and power reinforce rather than undermine one another.

Finally, Wildavsky addresses the role of citizens in public policy making. Citizen participation as a discrete element in the policy-making process has been a neglected topic, although the peripheral importance of citizenship has been examined in great detail. Wildavsky posits that "[b]y helping make what citizens learn in their daily lives part of what they need to know, analysis can improve both citizenship and public policy." Clearly, citizens cannot hope to fully participate in every public policy decision made by government. However, by specializing in issues about which individuals have a special interest, they sometimes can have an impact on public policy. Effectiveness as an "issue specialist" must be buttressed by a learning process through which a would-be specialist selects an issue, gathers information, shares information with other individuals with similar interests, and then acts. Although specialists may initially be motivated by self-interest, their interaction with others can enhance mutual interests by pointing out what others prefer and are willing to give up. Such a learning process can lead to changes in relationships among participants.

Most analyses of public policy assume the continuance of social and political relationships. Usually, changes sought do not constitute a complete rejection of the past. This is not to say that radical change cannot occur, because it can be the result of an accumulation of more modest changes. An enhanced role for citizens will not necessarily alter the conservative nature of public policy. The more policy issues and areas of a policy analysis that citizens are invited to participate in, however, the less likely they may be to participate in any. Wildavsky concludes that citizens as analysts will probably not alter the magnitude of change, but instead will certainly affect the quality of change (1987).

NEW THEORIES: POST-POSITIVIST PARTICIPATORY APPROACHES TO POLICY ANALYSIS

Wildavsky's early commentary on the need to increase social interaction in public policy analysis heralded what, a decade later, is called the post-positivist response to rationality in policy analysis. In general, post-positivism in the policy context consists of "value-critical" analysis coupled with an emphasis on participation and dialogue. The post-positivist movement sprang from the sense that policy studies were overly technical, perpetuated a fact–value dichotomy, presented precise numerical analysis when it was often inappropriate, and emphasized statistics that were themselves perceived to be easily manipulated by government agencies. Additionally, policy studies of this sort were used to confirm or oppose positions that had already been decided, were usually completed after the fact, and were plagued with inadequate performance (DeLeon, 1994a). The post-positivist response takes two forms. The first is to call for more participatory analysis while the second involves a reliance on critical theory. These new forms of analysis emphasize the importance of values within the context of discourse.

Participatory Policy Analysis

Frequently, those likely to be the most affected by new or revised policies are not consulted. Likewise, policy analysts are usually quite distant from the ultimate "targets" of their work. This state of affairs, as pointed out by DeLeon (1994a), is often the reason for the failure of many policy initiatives. To combat these tendencies, DeLeon and others suggest the antidote of participatory policy analysis.

Participatory policy analysis advocates and seeks out public opinion through a reliance on polling. The analyst randomly selects, educates, and listens to a selection of citizens and then tallies their views in such a way that they can be incorporated into the analysis. Policy polling, as envisioned by DeLeon, differs from other types of opinion polls in that the participants in policy polling serve as an actual decision making forum (like a legislature) whereas in most deliberative policy polls, participants function in an advisory role in terms of the suggestions they provide policy makers. To maximize the impact of public participation and to ensure that the views tallied represent the actual views and values of the affected citizenry, participatory policy analysis is consciously designed to incorporate the views of carefully selected, informed participants rather than reactively incorporate the views of self-selected elites or established interest groups (DeLeon, 1994a).

Participatory policy analysis poses several challenges, such as how to recruit participants, how to educate them once selected, and how to manage the entire process within the short time frame of most policy analyses. These are daunting problems. Few efforts have been made to actually use these techniques on a national level. DeLeon concludes that participatory policy analysis, emphasizing policy polling, is a way to identify and reach out to targeted stakeholders (as opposed to the general population).

Participatory Expertise

Fischer (1993a) has examined the interactions between policy analysts and those affected by policy decisions. Unlike the commentators cited above, Fischer has moved the debate from the purely theoretical to practical terms.

He initially characterizes the relationship between analysts and those who are affected by policy as a professional relationship much as in law and medicine with the analyst as the professional/ practitioner and those affected by a policy decision as the client. The analyst as professional is then cast as a mediator between interest groups and political representatives. This "superior–subordinate" relationship presumes that analysts conduct policy studies autonomously, and clients passively accept the results. Such a relationship inevitably leads to an assumption of "value-neutrality," precisely the concept that engenders the concern of post-positivists. Fischer's formulation of participatory policy analysis as "participatory expertise" is one way to deal with this concern.

Participatory expertise shifts the practitioner–client relationship to more of a collaborative relationship. In this new "client-centered" relationship, dialogue plays a crucial role. Fischer (1993a) outlines four factors essential to this client-centered relationship:

- Joint efforts of citizens and experts
- Spirit of inquiry and sharing of data
- Opportunity to influence each other
- Freedom to discontinue the relationship

Although many may view this approach as a messy, multimethod approach, Fischer responds by noting that this type of policy analysis is best suited to situations where the problem consists of a mix of technical and social problems, that the approach is really the scientific method made more time consuming, and that participatory expertise may hold the key to solving specific types of complex problems, namely those that pose challenges with no solutions or only temporary or imperfect solutions. One such example would be the problem faced by decision makers trying to site hazardous waste disposal facilities.

Hazardous waste disposal facility siting has often been approached by using formal assessments of risk to allay the "irrational" fears (not in my backyard [NIMBY] syndrome) of those most affected by such decisions. This approach has been largely unsuccessful and has led to a virtual stalemate in the siting of new waste disposal facilities. However, a different approach was used in Alberta, Canada (Swan Hills—opened September 11, 1987) to address opposition to the siting of a hazardous waste incinerator. Public participation was incorporated into the analysis from the outset. Stakeholders were given funds to hire their own experts and consultants, and meetings were held to discuss the proposed plan and its consequences (Paehlke & Torgerson, 1992). In other words, emphasis was placed on joint fact finding and consensus building. Once the siting of the incinerator was agreed to, meetings and seminars were held to educate the community. A local committee played an oversight function by reviewing the facility's monthly monitoring report. As the committee members gained expertise, the oversight function evolved into an enhanced deliberative relationship.

This example suggests that participatory policy analysis can be effective as an approach to dealing with a specific class or type of policy problem. Also, it is critical to note that technical expertise was not compromised in the name of an enhanced democratic process. Instead, collaborative negotiation and consensus building helped provide a solution to a particular environmental policy problem (Susskind & Laws, 1994).

Critical Theory

An alternative response to the post-positivist criticism of scientific policy analysis is critical theory. Critical theory posits that there are many perspectives that can and should be taken into account in any policy analysis; the scientific approach is just one of these. In addition, critical theory asserts that a fundamental asymmetry of knowledge and communicative styles is the basic reason for the failure of many policy analyses to lead to policy changes, and that institutional changes are required to enhance communication by challenging the natural conservatism of institutions (DeLeon, 1994a).

Forester develops a critical theory approach focusing on the use of practitioner stories to enhance communication and provide alternative perspectives to the problems addressed in policy analysis (Forester, 1993). The time demands placed on analysts frequently allow little time for systematic experimentation. Through practitioner stories, policy analysts can increase their experience regarding problems and conflicts in the world in which they work. In a practical setting, practitioner stories allow policy analysts to find out what has worked. This can provide a more informal basis for professionals to make judgments on what is valuable and significant.

Analogizing the telling of stories among practitioners to the telling of stories between friends, Forester notes that: (1) friends usually relate appropriate stories that bring knowledge, empathy, thoughtfulness, and insight to bear on a particular situation; (2) friends relate stories that use new words which in turn allow us to learn about our own insights, cares, and constraints in new ways; (3) friends do not usually offer cure-alls or technical fixes; (4) friends help us deliberate; and (5) friends present stories to us that are full of experience and passion, which prompt us not only to see consequences, but also to recognize "the demands, the vulnerabilities and precarious virtues required of a politically attentive, participatory professional practice" (Forester, 1993). In this sense, practitioner stories—as with stories between friends—help the analyst not only to focus and recognize views and judgments already maintained, but to see alternative perspectives and possibilities.

Of course, practitioner stories do not provide rules for all situations, and the inherent "messiness" of such stories teaches the analyst that problems must be properly formulated before solutions will become clear. Forester's approach to telling practitioner stories is similar to the approach used in this book of presenting examples of the effective use of environ-mental policy studies as a means of learning from past experience.

Forester's value critical approach actually addresses only the first two elements of critical theory: the advantages to taking many different per-spectives into account when conducting policy studies, and bridging the gap between knowledge and communication. The third element—altering institutional structures to combat the natural conservatism of policy analysis—is not required in Forester's approach. As Wildavsky pointed out, citizen participation (improved communication) enhances the qual-ity of change, not the quantity. Thus the third element is not crucial for the post-positivist approach to address the perceived limitations of the scientific approach to policy studies.

BEYOND PARTICIPATION—NETWORKS, COALITIONS, AND COMMUNITIES

Participatory theories of public policy analysis have recently given ground to still another array of approaches to better understanding public policy analysis. These three related concepts—policy networks, advocacy coali-tions, and epistemic communities—recognize that public policy analysis and decision making are influenced by a wide constellation of actors who interact both formally and informally. All three involve attempts to de-scribe these interactions and build theories around them.

Policy Networks

The concept of policy networks grows out of the realization that public policy analysis is affected by a variety of different actors. Bressers, O'Toole, and Richardson (1994) use the term *policy network* to denote "the large class of multi-actor [predominantly nongovernmental] arrangements of interdependencies in [the] varied phases of the policy process." Policy net-works can also be thought of as specific structural arrangements in policy making (Kenis & Schneider, 1991). Thus, policy networks are defined by their structure as inter-organizational arrangements, as well as by their function in the formulation and implementation of policy (Marin & Mayntz, 1991).

Early formulations of policy network analysis described "iron triangles" that depicted the relationship between executive agencies, congressional subcommittees, and interest groups in the public policy process. Later, the concept of policy networks was broadened to include other actors with indirect influence, thus leading to more loosely knit alliances (Dowding, 1995). Further research has focused on issue networks, specific policy networks that have developed around individual policy issues (Klijn, Koppenjan, & Termee, 1995).

Policy networks are described by their actors, linkages, and boundaries (Kenis & Schneider, 1991). Policy network analysis consists of sociological network analysis (primarily quantitative) and the other public policy analysis (mostly qualitative), and their integration (Marin & Mayntz, 1991).

Sociological networks can be viewed from two perspectives. The first concentrates on the structural aspects of the network itself and attempts to ascertain the relational characteristics among individual members by addressing the following factors (Dowding, 1995):

- Centrality
- Number of connections
- Inclusiveness
- Rules of interaction
- Embeddedness

The second concentrates on the actors themselves and Dowding (1995) characterizes them using:

- Knowledge and information
- Legitimacy
- Ability to influence (conditionally) other actors' incentive structure
- Ability to influence (unconditionally) other actors' incentive structure
- Reputation

The power of each actor is determined by the power of other actors in the network and their relationships. Similarly, the actors' relationships depend on their resources (Dowding, 1995). Dowding observes that sociological network analysis has been used to: (1) better define the relationship among actors within a given network and their individual characteristics as members of society; (2) study the relationship among actors' behaviors and a given network relationship; (3) study the relationship among the behavior of a group of actors and the network within which the group operates; and

(4) study the relationships among network configurations and the flow of information.

Policy network analysis attempts to take the work of sociological network analysis and superimpose it on the public policy domain. While most approaches to policy network analyses share a number of similar characteristics, they differ in important ways:

- Some focus on formal policy networks (Dowding, 1995) while others emphasize informal policy networks (Marin & Mayntz, 1991).
- Some focus on individual actors and their bargaining characteristics (Dowding. 1995) while others stress the actors' respective organizations and organizational identities (Bressers, O'Toole, & Richardson, 1994).
- Some focus on informal, decentralized, and horizontal relations in the policy process (Kenis & Schneider, 1991) while others emphasize the collective actions of organized actors and interorganizational relations in the public policy process (Marin & Mayntz, 1991).
- There is a limit to the utility of policy network analysis. It is good for describing the relationships among actors but not so effective for deriving causal explanations in structural terms (Dowding, 1995). Policy network analysis provides a valuable tool for allowing governmental and administrative actors to better manage policy networks (Klijn et al., 1995), and policy network analysis provides a powerful tool to study highly complex structure in modern politics (Kenis and Schneider, 1991).

Although policy network analysis does not provide a coherent theory of public policy formulation and implementation, proponents of the policy network approach argue that continued study is important because the world is increasingly "networked," and policy network analysis provides an important analytical tool for better understanding the policy process (Bressers, O'Toole, & Richardson, 1994). Dowding (1995) counters by arguing that although policy network analysis can effectively describe a policy network, its actors, and relationships, it does little to explain the policy process because it cannot be ascertained whether government agents acted as interested participants, disinterested intermediaries, or were "captured by certain groups."

Beyond its analytical strengths, Klijn et al. (1995) argues that policy network analysis can be used by government organizations to manage complex networks of stakeholders and to provide criteria for the assessment and improvement of networks. Kenis and Schneider (1991) argue that policy network analysis can be used to

- compare networks regarding the prospects for cooperation and coordination in the policy process,
- conduct cross-network comparisons to develop hypotheses explaining the effect of aggregation on specific interactions,
- develop and test formal models of the policy-making process,
- test hypotheses including structural propositions,
- identify and reconstruct the relations or patterns of actions between actors in the formulation and implementation of a policy, and
- reconstruct network dynamics in terms of structural transformation or stability.

Despite this positive outlook, the reality is that it is often difficult to fully identify all of the actors and relationships in a particular policy or issue network. In the meantime, policy network analysis does generate academic interest both nationally and internationally.

Advocacy Coalition Framework

Sabatier and Jenkins-Smith (1993) have developed the advocacy coalition framework (ACF) to explain the emergence of particular public policies. They contend that competing advocacy coalitions form around specific policy subsystems, and that these advocacy coalitions are composed of diverse sets of actors from both the public and the private spheres, including multiple layers of government, and have a core set of beliefs in common. These core beliefs tend to be stable and hold coalitions together (e.g., environmental concerns must be considered of equal importance to economic concerns, or market forces should determine levels of environmental protection, etc.). These core beliefs and the dominance of certain coalitions over others, can usually only be changed by external pressures from outside the policy subsystem.

Advocacy coalitions also share secondary beliefs regarding the way core beliefs should be implemented. These are more likely to change and may vary somewhat over time. Policy-oriented learning between advocacy coalitions or between advocacy coalitions and "policy brokers" can influence secondary beliefs within a coalition, leading to policy change. Even secondary beliefs, however, are not likely to be changed immediately by an evaluation or some other analysis, but instead change gradually over time (Sabatier & Jenkins-Smith suggest a decade or more as the proper time frame) as new information is presented and integrated into the belief system. Fundamental change will occur only if significant forces outside the policy subsystem change the composition, influence, or beliefs of actors within the subsystem. Sabatier and Jenkins-Smith also make a distinction between "purposive" and "material" groups. Purposive groups are centered on core beliefs, and view interests (comparable to secondary beliefs) as being flexible as long as their core beliefs are sustained. Material groups, on the other hand, are focused on immediate interests, and core beliefs are of less importance as long as their interests are met. Material groups may be willing to abandon their core beliefs if it serves their material interests to do so. Therefore, core beliefs for material groups will tend to be less stable than those for other groups.

Although the advocacy coalition approach has generated enormous interest because it concentrates on the importance of ideas and their origins in policy analysis, several commentators are quite critical. Dowding (1995) argues that because the advocacy coalition approach centers on beliefs as instigators of policy change, it forces attention away from the concept of knowledge as power and away from the idea of viewing policy change as a consequence of ideological battles between groups. Therefore, by concentrating on two causes of policy change (values of coalition members and shocks to the system) the advocacy coalition approach fails to address how such ideas "can be used and misused by other agencies." Schlager (1995) takes a more positive stance suggesting that the advocacy coalition approach can benefit from more thoroughly considering how coalitions form and maintain themselves over time and the strategies they use to achieve their goals. Even Dowding maintains that the advocacy coalition approach, taken together with institutional rational choice theory (discussed above) "may prove one of the most useful theories of the policy process."

Epistemic Communities

Advocacy coalition frameworks have been faulted for failing to recognize the power of knowledge in public policy analysis. The concept of epistemic communities cedes knowledge center stage and demonstrates its importance in policy innovation, particularly in the area of international policy making.

Haas (1992b) defines an epistemic community as "a network of professionals with recognized expertise and competence in a particular domain and an authoritative claim to policy-relevant knowledge within that domain or issue area." The professionals making up an epistemic community may come from different backgrounds and disciplines; however, they have in common the following characteristics:

- Shared beliefs (normative and principled), which provide a value-based rationale for the actions of members
- Shared causal beliefs derived from their expertise and past practice concerning problems in their domain, which in turn serves as a foundation for discovering linkages between possible policy actions and desired outcomes
- Shared notions of validity, which establish criteria for weighing and validating knowledge within their domain of expertise
- Common policy enterprise, which defines a set of common practices directed toward the policy problems in their domain of expertise

Epistemic communities are distinguished from other policy actors and policy groups as outlined in Figure 5-3.

		Causal Beliefs		Knowledge Base	
		Shared	Unshared	Consensual	Disputed or Absent
Principled	Shared	Epistemic Communities	Interest Groups and Social Movements		
Beliefs	Unshared	Disciplines and Professionals	Legislators, Bureaucratic Agencies, and Bureaucratic Coalitions		
Interests	Shared			Epistemic Communities	Interest Groups, Social Movements, and Bureaucratic Coalitions
	Unshared			Disciplines and Professionals	Legislators and Bureaucratic Agencies

Figure 5-3. Distinguishing Epistemic Communities from Other Groups.
(Haas, 1992b).

A good example of an environmentally related epistemic community is the ecological epistemic community, which was responsible for framing the international debate on ozone depleting chemical emissions—specifically chlorofluorocarbons (CFCs). The ecological epistemic community was composed of atmospheric scientists and like-minded policy makers. They shared a common set of values—preserving the quality of the environment—and accepted the causal analysis that CFC emissions were responsible for destroying the earth's ozone layer. Their policy enterprise consisted of preserving the earth's ozone layer. Finally, they shared common validity tests based on the scientific method. The result of their efforts was the enactment of the Montreal Protocol on Substances That Deplete the Ozone Layer in 1987 (Haas, 1992a).

The basis of any epistemic community is consensual knowledge (not guesses or raw data), which is the product of human interpretation. It is not necessarily the truth. The focus of the epistemic community approach is to reach consensus in a particular area and then diffuse that information to other actors. The members of an epistemic community focus on the practical influence they can have on collective decision making rather than concentrating on generating truth. The diffusion of knowledge occurs when epistemic community members educate decision makers as to problems and assist decision makers in identifying state interests, and when decision makers solicit their views and delegate responsibility to them. As such, epistemic communities can be viewed as an extranational "force" working to develop intellectual consensus among state interests. The epistemic community approach to the diffusion of knowledge suggests a nonsystemic origin of state interests and identifies the dynamic of cooperation outside existing power structures. As such, epistemic communities can be most effective in situations involving uncertainty and when state interests are not clearly apparent (Haas, 1992b).

Epistemic communities are viewed as generators of policy innovation. Their policy ideas evolve independent of government influence, and they act independently of the policies of the top leaders of their respective governments (Haas, 1992b). Thus they may present new patterns of reasoning or new courses of action to decision makers, which in turn may lead to unpredicted outcomes (Adler & Haas, 1992).

Adler and Haas (1992) note that epistemic communities can influence international policy innovation by

- framing the range of a political controversy surrounding an issue (e.g., ecological epistemic community with respect to CFCs),
- defining state interests, and
- setting standards.

Once their ideas are adopted, epistemic communities continue to influence state policy practice in that area via institutional habit and inertia.

The epistemic communities approach has been criticized from several directions. Sebenius (1992) argues that although epistemic communities influence policy through bargaining, there is no theory of bargaining described in the approach. More specifically, the emphasis of the epistemic approach has been to identify communities, their members, and their positions, rather than to systematically discuss the mechanism by which epistemic community members translate their beliefs and preferences into influence over policy outcomes. A deeper problem with epistemic communities is the disproportionate power that is presumably given to an ad hoc group of appointed bureaucrats to influence critical global decisions and the apparent lack of "national interest" exhibited by community members (Susskind, 1994).

Dowding (1995) argues that, fundamentally, epistemic communities want to see their belief systems lead to policy convergence rather than viewing international agreements as the result of power bargaining between self-interested nations. Baark and Strahl (1995) argue that, although the epistemic communities approach may explain coordination and convergence on policy issues among nations, it has not been very effective in changing the policy agenda of specific international organizations

Seemingly, epistemic communities have been effective in addressing international environmental policy making, particularly in situations where there is great uncertainty as to proper policy directions. Narum (1993) even expresses the hope that epistemic communities in the environmental field can be critical players in establishing the rights of future generations in international environmental policy decisions and agreements. It is not quite clear how to test these propositions or whether they will apply in other policy-making contexts.

CONCLUDING REMARKS

The material presented in this chapter traces the development and evolution of policy sciences over the course of this century. Policy science, viewed by Lasswell as a means of enhancing the democratic process, shifted to predominantly rational or scientific approaches, which relied on a notion of "value-neutral" analysis. The successes or failures of these analyses were increasingly seen as driven by institutional and hierarchical forces. Newer approaches, which ostensibly attempt to bring policy science back in line with Lasswell's ideals, all but reject the notion of scientific analysis in favor of approaches that stress enhanced communication (e.g., rhetorical methods, as discussed in Chapter 6) and focus on institutional influences on the individual within the policy-making process. Our conclusion is that there is still a need for scientific policy analysis—particularly in the area of environmental policy making—but that we have reached a point where it is both possible and necessary to integrate, as Wildavsky would say, intelligence and social interaction.

Rethinking the Choice of Methods for Policy Analysis

The theories discussed in Chapter 5 suggest three overlapping sets of methods for conducting environmental policy studies: analytical methods, rhetorical methods, and process methods. We examine each in turn, relating them to the six examples of effective environmental policy studies discussed in Chapter 3. In light of this examination, we then turn once again to Congressman Randolph's concern about the continued use of chlorinated organic compounds.

ANALYTICAL METHODS

Analytical methods usually involve a *systematic, scientific approach to the development of policy options.* Examples include cost–benefit analyses, risk assessments, gaming simulation, and linear and dynamic modeling. More often than not, using analytical methods in environmental policy studies involves a heavy reliance on the rational approaches to policy studies outlined in Chapter 5—particularly systems analysis. Although our review of the topic in Chapter 5 might lead the reader to believe that purely analytical policy methods have fallen out of favor, these techniques have in fact been successfully employed in studies such as *Lead in Gasoline* and the *Delaney Paradox.* Indeed, there are situations in which purely analytical methods present the only practical approach. Moreover, Arrow et al. (1996) argue that cost–benefit analysis should be incorporated into every policy analysis involving environmental, health, and safety questions tied to modification or adoption of regulations.

When an analyst opts to use an analytical approach to developing policy options, there are several factors that determine the effectiveness of the ensuing environmental policy study. First, as seemingly straightforward as analytical methods appear to be, values inevitably influence the outcome of the analysis and must be handled carefully. Rein (1976) refers to these values as "frames," and posits that "[i]nformation and data can never be understood in isolation from the context of ideas which give them meaning." In other words, information and data are not value-neutral. A study may be valid and consistent in terms of internal criteria, but still may be opposed by those whose interests it affects. The crucial point, argues Rein, is that questions of interpretation rather than matters of fact often shape policy debates. Claims of causality underlying a policy issue are often unclear and open to competing interpretations. The data and information used in an environmental policy study will, therefore, have a critical influence on the results. Different sets of data, all equally valid, employed in the same analytical way can nevertheless produce results that vary considerably. Eberstadt (1995) illustrates this phenomenon by examining a number of different public policy studies (and resulting policy decisions) to demonstrate how using different parameters and different sets of data (emphasizing alternative causal factors) yield starkly contrasting results.

Second, each analytical method rests on assumptions and values that must be understood prior to its use in a policy study. A risk assessment, for example, usually assumes that risks below a certain threshold will be acceptable. In a cost–benefit analysis, although costs are usually quantifiable, benefits often are not. Certain assumptions must be made about what the benefits are and how they are to be quantified. Hendrickson, Lave, and McMichael (1995) illustrate this point quite nicely in their analysis of the recycling program in Pittsburgh, Pennsylvania, discussed in Chapter 4. Perceived benefits from the recycling program included income generation, resource conservation, and environmental benefits in general. However, upon deeper analysis, Hendrickson, Lave, & McMichael (1995) demonstrated that disposing of recyclables was actually more expensive than dumping in a landfill and required a disproportionate amount of resources to collect recyclables. Far from benefiting the environment, the recycling program appeared to cause more harm to the environment. Apart from these quantifiable benefits, the authors were unable to evaluate factors like social benefits and other similar intangibles, clearly demonstrating some of the barriers to employing cost–benefit analysis.

Third, the assumptions and values discussed must be made explicit at the outset of the study. Although opponents may argue the validity of particular assumptions and values, stating them "up front" lends credibility to a study. For example, if risk assessment is involved, the analyst should specify at the outset the level below which risks will be deemed acceptable, and study results should indicate whether the risks were in fact below that level. Similarly, credibility depends on whether benefits are identified at the outset of a study in which cost–benefit analysis is used.

Finally, analysts should share all their data and results with others in the field and across disciplines. This enhances the credibility of their work and encourages future studies by opening up causal connections or avenues previously unexplored to independent scrutiny. This is particularly important in the environmental field, where interactions among various disciplines are hard to maintain.

The ways in which these approaches to handling methodological difficulties can enhance the effectiveness of analytical policy studies are evident in both *Lead in Gasoline* and the *Delaney Paradox*.

Lead in Gasoline

As we discussed in Chapter 3, the *Lead in Gasoline* study relied on cost–benefit analysis. At the outset, Environmental Protection Agency (EPA) analysts were able to identify a clear benefit associated with reducing lead: The reduction of human lead intake reduced the incidence of high blood pressure. Once this benefit was identified and quantified, it could be tied to the cost of reducing lead levels in gasoline. The results were staggering. The significance and credibility of the "benefit" were identified as the primary factors leading to the adoption of regulations lowering lead levels in gasoline.

The *Delaney Paradox*

The *Delaney Paradox* study employed risk assessment methods that examined pesticide levels in raw and processed foods. Acceptable levels of risk were identified at the outset, lending credibility to the resulting policy recommendation that a consistent negligible risk standard be adopted for pesticides in both raw and processed foods. Additionally, analysts subjected the findings and conclusions of the study to a broad peer review process and ultimately incorporated much of the resulting feedback into the final report. The credibility of the study in the eyes of Congress and the Clinton administration was clear. This led to the statutory adoption of a uniform negligible risk standard for pesticide levels in raw and processed foods.

RHETORICAL METHODS

Rhetorical methods represent another approach to conducting environmental policy studies. Rhetorical methods involve *persuasion, advocacy,* and *consensus building.* Although rhetorical approaches emphasize persuasion, analytical methods also play a role in providing convincing evidence to support policy recommendations. Rhetorical methods are most appropriate when a study concerns broad changes in policy direction or when many stakeholders will ultimately feel the impact of proposed changes in policy. Examples of rhetorical methods include risk communication and meta–policy analyses such as those used in the *Reducing Risk* study.

Because rhetorical approaches focus on persuasion, it is important that policy analysts incorporate the following techniques into their analyses. First, analysts should put together data in a convincing fashion. To accomplish this, analysts must first identify the primary audience of their study—those who need to be persuaded. Obviously, decision makers constitute one such audience. However, when the audience is much larger and composed primarily of lay people, the use of risk communication strategies such as public disclosure, educating the media and the public about the issues, and maintaining a channel for communication by interested stakeholders, is important. When this is the case, Morgan et al. (1992) argue that it is imperative that data be presented in such a way that lay individuals can understand them and use them to make rational decisions. Morgan et al. suggest that this can be accomplished with a four-step process:

1. Elicit people's beliefs, both accurate and inaccurate about a hazard.
2. Ascertain the prevalence of these beliefs.
3. Develop communications, based on the information gathered in the first two steps, to inform people of what they need to know to make informed decisions.
4. Test the effectiveness of the communications strategy adopted.

When the prospective audience is an executive agency, different strategies of persuasion will often make more sense. Williams (1987), a policy analyst at the Rand Corporation, notes that when using rhetorical approaches to policy analysis, it is imperative to know your audience, and to recognize that facts don't speak for themselves and that timing is everything.

Second, the study should be organized to appeal to commonly held democratic values. If such values are only implied, decision makers may not make the connection between the study results and the underlying values they represent. By making these values explicit, a study is more likely to persuade decision makers to take action. Additionally, explicit reference to democratically held values is particularly relevant to environmental policy studies where issues often defy attempts at quantification and the "economically most efficient" solution may not be the fairest (Susskind & Cruikshank, 1987).

Third, analysts should illustrate their arguments with actual cases. Forester (1993) argues that the use of practice-based stories can assist analysts in conducting policy studies. Similarly, stories of actual cases can be incorporated into a presentation of findings to demonstrate the practical reality of a particular argument. The cases selected can be "success stories" chosen to bolster a particular policy recommendation, or cases that illustrate the gravity of an issue, highlighting the need to take action.

Finally, analysts should build on the work of well-respected experts. Often, the impact of recommendations will be based not so much on what the analyst says, but on who supports them. The critical consideration here is trust. Especially in environmental policy studies, data are often complex and difficult to understand. Additionally, as Rein (1976) points out, data frequently lend themselves to alternative interpretations. The decision maker may ultimately be unable or unwilling to completely trust the arguments presented in the analysis. However, the decision maker may be more willing to trust recognized and well-respected experts who make the same arguments or lend their support to study results and recommendations. Relying on well-respected experts to conduct or review study results represents one more approach to enhancing the persuasiveness and thus the effectiveness of a policy study.

A good example of an effective environmental policy study that benefited from use of rhetorical methods is the *Reducing Risk* study discussed in Chapter 3.

Reducing Risk

The *Reducing Risk* analysis undertook a daunting task—to generate recommendations concerning prioritizing environmental efforts at the EPA. The scope of the study (referred to as a meta–policy analysis) was broad and its recommendations implicated all of EPA, as well as other agencies, states, and individuals. A rhetorical method was called for in order to persuade EPA that policy recommendations aimed at reconciling conflicting agency mandates were important. The study argued that equal attention should be paid to ecological and human health risks. The study employed over 60 EPA Science Advisory Board (SAB) members and more than 250 experts to bolster its findings.

The study, in fact, persuaded EPA to alter its long-term risk reduction strategy and to reorganize appropriately.

PROCESS METHODS

Process methods represent a third approach to environmental policy studies. Process methods involve *public participation* and *consensus building among affected stakeholding interests.* At times, such participation may be purely advisory, while at other times, participants may form a partnership with analysts in developing study results (Susskind & Field, 1996). They also involve situations that call for analyses across more than one discipline. Process methods bridge the gap between the differing opinions of interested parties as well as the contributions of different disciplines. While rhetorical approaches target situations where the study will affect large numbers of stakeholders, process methods are particularly useful in situations involving smaller numbers of individuals or a more easily defined region. Good examples of process methods include public participation and interdisciplinary collaboration.

The *Alternative Agricultural Research and Commercialization (AARC)* and *Spotted Owl* studies illustrate how process methods can be effectively used in environmental policy studies.

AARC

Fischer (1993a) demonstrates how the joint participation of experts and stakeholders can be effectively employed in a study of an environmental policy problem that generally has no ideal solutions, such as the siting of a waste treatment facility. The *AARC* study demonstrates that if stakeholder representatives are incorporated in a collaborative study, they are more likely to accept the technical basis for the eventual decision, even though they may still disapprove of it. *AARC* task force members included representatives of industry, the public sector, and academia. Although the study was noticeably short on scientific support, the process employed helped to identify many of the roadblocks to commercialization of new agricultural products and processes. Such a result would probably not have been possible if interested parties had not been included in the analysis. The study ultimately resulted in legislation that established the *AARC*. Perhaps because of the direct involvement of so many interests, the *AARC* has successfully operated for over a decade as envisioned by the study participants.

Spotted Owl

The problems addressed in the *Spotted Owl* study could have been addressed as nothing more than a tradeoff between ecological protection (owls) and economic growth (jobs). However, the strength of the study was that it adopted an interdisciplinary perspective, redefining the critical question as one of ecosystem management. In this way, analysts not only addressed the issue of owl preservation, but also the related topics of information gathering and analysis, watershed restoration, and prescribed burning. The process methods employed by the analysts thus facilitated the synthesis of information from a wide range of disciplines. This powerful form of interdisciplinary analysis allowed the analysts to present fourteen separate policy options, each characterized by data viewed as accurate, from which Congress could choose.

PUTTING IT ALL TOGETHER: THE ISSUE OF CHLORINATED ORGANIC COMPOUNDS REVISITED

The three sets of methods discussed here—analytical, rhetorical, and process methods—provide a convenient framework for thinking about how to approach tough environmental policy questions. All of the factors discussed in earlier chapters will come into play in deciding on a method or combination of methods to employ, which uses to target, and what organizational strategy to rely on in carrying out an environmental policy study.

If we shift back to the concerns of Congressman Randolph—the environmental and human health risks posed by the continued use of chlorinated organic compounds, we can see the way that each of the three sets of methods might come into play. As Congressman Randolph pointed out, many different groups have conducted studies concerning the various aspects of the chlorinated organic compound issue. The sponsors of these studies are diverse and include environmental groups, health groups, industrial and trade groups, and government advisory bodies. The issue has been addressed at the national, regional, and state level. And not unexpectedly, the results and recommendations of these studies have been in conflict with each other.

There are a number of factors that Congressman Randolph must weigh when deciding which method to pursue. Any of the three approaches or a combination could result in a credible and effective environmental policy study.

First, he must be politically circumspect. Given a politically charged climate, he should be focused on generating the highest possible degree of legitimacy. As we discussed in Chapter 2, it is not difficult to find and hire a consultant to produce a report along the lines you desire. Whether decision makers pay attention to the results of such a study, however, will hinge in large part on the degree of legitimacy the study achieves. Because there are already so many published studies concerning the continued use of chlorinated organic compounds, only a new study with an extraordinarily high degree of legitimacy will influence decision makers. In addition, timing is crucial. A study that arrives after decision makers have formulated and announced their positions will have little or no impact. Thus, the selection of a method or set of methods that requires coordination with various stakeholders before recommendations can be formulated may not be appropriate when a decision must be reached quickly. Finally, fiscal constraints and organizational constraints can also shift the preference for one approach over another. Optimizing these factors and others should result in the selection of a method or approach by the analysts considering the needs of the sponsor and nature of the study and will hopefully produce an effective environmental policy analysis.

ENHANCING THE INTERPLAY OF
THEORY AND PRACTICE

In previous sections, we discussed the various theories of public policy analysis as well as the methods that can enhance the effectiveness of environmental policy studies. In this section, we focus on the interaction of knowledge and learning in environmental policy, the importance of science in environmental policy making, and what the future might hold in terms of new theories and methods for environmental policy analyses.

Knowledge and Learning in Environmental Policy Making

We have discussed how knowledge relates to power (Wildavsky, 1987), how knowledge is disseminated, and how information and data, depending on the perspective they are viewed from, often affect the outcome of policy analyses (Rein, 1976). Environmental policy analysis frequently calls for the interaction of many interested parties, for example, government agencies and decision makers (wishing to redirect public processes in a particular direction), stakeholders (those affected by any policy decision), other interested groups, and those who are involved in implementing selected policies. Environmental policy analysis and policy making increasingly involve collective action (Loeber, 1996). Loeber argues that because "analysis in practice does not provide a neutral, unbiased and impartial input into (political) decision making, it is relevant to consider the impact of the activity of analysis itself on the policy process." Sabatier and Jenkins-Smith (1993) use the term *policy-oriented learning* to describe the concept of considering changes over time regarding the distribution of policy knowledge and policy positions of the various groups involved in the policy analysis and policy-making process. Consequently, the role of analytical debate in policy-oriented learning is essentially characterized by the way analysis is employed (Loeber, 1996).

Loeber notes that an effective way to attack the collective action problem in environmental policy analysis is to (1) include the perspectives of the various actors in the policy-making process in the policy analysis itself, and (2) select an approach to analysis that is interactive and interpretive in character. Many of these approaches have been discussed in Chapter 5 (e.g., participatory policy analysis and critical theory). Loeber continues that in order to make collective action work, new information must be systematically made available to all of the individuals involved in the policy analysis. This allows the various actors to reflect on each others' points of view and underlying assumptions.

One type of policy-oriented learning occurs in professional and open forums. A professional forum, much like an epistemic community, consists of participants who have a common basis for assessing analytical claims. The drawbacks of professional forums include: (1) the forum may represent only a small cluster of actors interested in particular environmental problems; and (2) the screening of forum participants can effectively eliminate those with opposing policy viewpoints. Open forums, on the other hand, consist of participants who do not share a common analytical basis. While they are more representative, open forums (1) are more likely to find themselves caught up in analytical conflicts, and (2) often do not provide a basis for achieving consensus on contentious policy issues (Sabatier & Jenkins-Smith, 1993). However, open forums can enhance learning among the various participants and lead to questioning of tacit assumptions or belief systems (Loeber, 1996). In fact, both types of forums can work—in real time as well as in cyberspace—as long as they are facilitated effectively by professional "neutrals"(Susskind, McKearnan, & Thomas-Larmer, 1999), operate under clear and appropriate ground rules, and build on a basis of shared technical analysis (Ozawa, 1991).

Although the present trend in environmental policy analysis appears to be toward collective action, we must not forget or neglect the importance of science in environmental policy analysis.

Role of Science and Technical Knowledge

Policy issues with complex scientific and technical ramifications naturally require scientific and technical input for effective policy analysis and wise policy formulation. Most environmental policy issues arise in complex economic, social, political, scientific, and technical contexts. Consequently, effective integration of these contexts in defining problems, identifying and evaluating policy alternatives, and arriving at policy options is essential. Brown (1993, p. 10) has suggested that

> [S]cience has been particularly effective at influencing policy debate when it is overtly linked to widely shared subjective values. Over the past 25 years, the remarkable success of the environmental movement in influencing national priorities has been due largely to the popularity of an

ethical or spiritual position [of preserving and protecting the environ-
ment] bolstered by scientific expertise.

Integrating scientific and technical considerations in policy analysis
and formulation poses many problems. The very nature of scientific inquiry—focusing on understanding fundamental mechanisms of physical,
biological, and social systems; experimentation, data collection, and
analysis; generating new knowledge and then making a credible scientific
case—dictates a considerable investment in time. Results are hardly ever
conclusive, as there are always some uncertainties. More research alone to
resolve uncertainties is rarely helpful. Indeed, as Brown (1993) suggests,
"the search for greater accuracy in science may lead to greater controversy in politics. Few would argue that dioxin is highly toxic; the exact
degree and nature of the toxicity, however, is subject to endless debate."
Additional research related to the effects of dioxin has not minimized the
controversy.

While the goal of science is objectivity, the goal of policy formulation is
to study all sides of an issue, build consensus, and formulate a policy that is
acceptable given what is known and not known. These goals at times may
seem to be at odds. What role can scientific and technical knowledge play
in policy formulation and how should scientific information be conveyed
to affect policy?

Scientific research can help anticipate potential problems that may result from selecting certain policy choices. Under conditions of uncertainty,
scientific and technical input can help devise contingent policy options
that permit action even if the future is not clear. Policy makers and the scientific and technical community can work together to design incremental,
adaptive policies that can move toward prescribed goals along multiple
and evolving pathways (Brown, 1993). Unfortunately, too much technical
information is conveyed to the public and policy makers in ways that are
not "user friendly." It is natural for scientific and technical personnel to
want to be precise, accurate, and comprehensive. But complicated, volumi-
nous, and untimely technical information often becomes incomprehensi-
ble, irrelevant, and marginally useful if no effort is made to present it
properly. Thus, scientific information has to be conveyed in a user-friendly
and timely manner.

Because there are enormous scientific and technical ramifications of
each environmental policy choice, it is prudent to involve those technically
competent in the examination of policy options. Such partnerships often

lead to what we have already noted—"joint fact-finding" (Ozawa, 1991). This mode of collective inquiry works best when all the stakeholding parties play a role in selecting a single set of technical advisers, specify the research protocol together, and use the services of a neutral interlocutor (Susskind, McKearnan, & Thomas-Larmer, 1999).

Policy Studies Can Often Raise More Questions

In previous chapters we have discussed the role of problem definition in environmental policy analysis and the need to define the problem in helpful ways. However, no matter how much effort is put into problem definition, the analysis itself will often raise more questions that need to be addressed. This is not necessarily a bad thing. Many environmental issues are quite complex. Causal connections and interactions are often poorly understood. As groups dig more deeply into an issue, and learning occurs, new questions are sure to arise.

New problems or questions can be handled in two ways. Some methods of analysis can incorporate refinements in problem definition. In the *Spotted Owl* study, for example, the analysts redefined the issue as one of ecosystem management, supplanting the narrower conception of jobs versus owls. Second, new issues raised can be addressed in subsequent policy analyses.

When the environmental issues are narrow, as in the *Spotted Owl* study, it may be possible to successfully adopt a wider problem definition. When an issue is quite complex, it may be necessary to tackle pieces of the problem in a creative manner. This approach was adopted in the *Reducing Risk* study where the SAB committee was divided into three subcommittees— Ecology and Welfare, Human Health, and Strategic Options—each of which issued a report that was then included in the main report as appendices. The resulting meta-policy approach facilitated analysis of three different policy issues on an individual basis at the outset, while addressing new issues raised at the later integration stage.

There Is Still Great Room for Progress

The problems and complexities associated with environmental policy management often seem daunting. In this book we have illustrated six effective environmental policy studies. However, there are countless other environmental policy efforts that have not been nearly as successful and indeed can be considered failures. Rubin, Lave, & Morgan (1992) illustrate the failure of the $500 million, decade-long National Acid Precipitation Assessment Program (NAPAP) to effect changes in the Clean Air Act in 1990. This well-funded, lengthy study, although producing a lot of "good" science, was not prepared in time for decision makers to use it in drafting the new Clean Air Act. Additionally, the information contained in its twenty-seven technical reports and three-volume integrated assessment was not presented in a manner that could be easily understood by the decision makers. The results of the NAPAP study highlight the institutional and organizational obstacles facing acceptance and implementation of study results.

The *Complex Cleanup* study highlights these obstacles as well. The Office of Technology Assessment (OTA) began the study by evaluating what was known about the contamination and public health problems at nuclear weapons facilities as well as the remediation technologies available to address them. However, the analysis and subsequent report instead focused on institutional changes that were needed. The study documented that the Department of Energy (DOE) did not have a process in place to collect information about public health impacts, lacked adequate public participation, and lost public credibility because of these practices and past behaviors. OTA concluded that the current institutional structure at DOE precluded making the proposed changes. In much the same way, Rubin, Lave, & Morgan (1992) conclude that organizational barriers precluded the NAPAP study from being an effective effort to address the complex issue of acid rain.

Environmental policy theorists and analysts are currently considering various strategies for addressing these complex institutional and organizational obstacles. One area of current research involves the use of integrated policy assessments, a policy analysis framework akin to a meta–policy analysis, where complex issues with large degrees of uncertainty can be addressed in a systematic, meaningful manner. Rubin et al. (1992) note that one of the primary reasons NAPAP failed to influence new clean air legislation was that there was no serious effort made to define policy related research priorities. If this had been done, it might have aided in setting appropriate research priorities and timetables. Integrated assessments offer an effective means of establishing a mechanism for reviewing the results of research and reevaluating research priorities. Integrated policy assessments seek to (1) survey the current state of knowledge concerning an issue under discussion, (2) reach scientifically informed judgments concerning what is known and not known as well as key uncertainties, and (3) ascertain where new research might aid the policy process most effectively. Integrated policy assessments thus form a bridge between the scientific and policy communities (Rubin, Lave, & Morgan, 1992).

To be credible, such assessments should be conducted simultaneously by several groups of researchers. One assessment should be conducted by a nongovernmental organization such as a university or a nonprofit research organization. A second, parallel assessment should be conducted in-house by the government. Dowlatabadi (1995) summarizes and describes three families of current integrated assessment models as follows:

- Cost-effectiveness framing (e.g., DGEM and MARKAL)
- Cost-impact framing (e.g., IMAGE)
- Cost–benefit framing (e.g., CETA and PAGE)

Dowlatabadi and Morgan (1993) argue that integrated policy assessment is essential to tackling complex, long-term environmental issues. Using such models to address research priorities can help overcome many of the institutional and organizational barriers to effective environmental policy analysis.

"Backward mapping" can be used to assess an implementing agency's organizational capability to pursue a policy option and to produce the desired result (Lynn, 1987). Backward mapping includes:

- Describing the problem behavior at the lowest level of implementation
- Determining the ability of the implementing organization to affect this target behavior
- Determining the resources the implementing organization will require in order to bring about the desired change in the target behavior
- Describing the policy that will produce these required resources

Although backward mapping may be useful to identify situations where the organization may not be capable of implementing a selected policy alternative, it offers few tools for modifying institutional and organizational structures to effectuate policy implementation.

The use of alternative policy instruments may provide a viable option for achieving policy goals (McDonnell & Elmore, 1987). Alternative policy instruments include:

- *Mandates*—rules that govern the actions of individuals and agencies and are intended to produce compliance

- *Inducements*—the transfer of money to individuals or agencies in return for certain types of actions
- *Capacity-building*—the transfer of money for the purpose of investment in material, intellectual, or human resources
- *System-changing*—the transfer of official authority among individuals and agencies.

Of the various alternative policy instruments presented, system-changing goes farthest toward hurdling the barriers posed by institutional and organizational obstacles.

Another approach to addressing institutional problems in environmental management was presented earlier when we discussed Wildavsky's "self-evaluating" organization. Wildavsky (1987) examines the role of knowledge and power within the construct of a model of a self-evaluating organization. Such an ideal organization would be one that continually monitored its own activities to determine not only how well it is meeting its objectives, but whether the objectives need to be changed. In Wildavsky's view, a self-evaluating organization uses its institutional or organizational structure to overcome many of the barriers identified above. The barriers to creating a self-evaluating organization include the mindset of the individuals in an organization and their "loyalty" to established clientele and ways of working, the tension between different programs within an organization, the tendency to disregard policy choices that appear ineffective (as opposed to analyzing why they were ineffective), and the resources (time and money) required to support evaluation. Wildavsky proposes that forward-thinking individuals within an organization who possess a willingness to critically evaluate current objectives and clientele in light of the future, however uncertain, can be a powerful engine for overcoming traditional institutional barriers. When needed, program managers can shift resources among projects instead of making absolute judgments as to which are better at a particular time. Program managers can also focus on why certain policy efforts are failing and what can be done to correct such failures. To accomplish such objectives requires a radical change in institutional thinking. Once organizational actors recognize the need for experimentation, select and gather relevant information for evaluation, and establish a basis of trust both within the organization as well as with external actors, the self-evaluating or learning organization will be much closer to becoming reality.

CONCLUDING REMARKS

Policy science continues to evolve. There is certainly room for progress. Theoretical approaches to environmental policy study need to be improved so that they better address the technical, economic, political, and cultural context in which policy is made. In practice, environmental policy studies confront institutional obstacles that we need to better understand. Finally, bridging the gap between theory and practice with respect to environmental policy making will require a set of highly trained policy analysts who understand both the uses and the organizational context of environmental policy studies.

7

International Perspectives

The principal focus of this book has been national environmental policy and the challenges associated with conducting policy studies and using study results. However, we are entering an era of globalization. As world population continues to grow, topping 6 billion in early 2000, and spills across borders, and as industries (and their emissions and effluents) spread beyond national boundaries, a focus on international environmental concerns will become critical. Although a number of international environmental treaties and conventions were generated during the late twentieth century, more will need to be written.

In this chapter, we provide a brief glimpse of the future challenges and possibilities involved in international environmental policy studies. A single chapter cannot do justice to this increasingly complex and important set of issues, but we hope at least to note some of the issues and strategies involved in environmental policy formulation in an international context, and to provide some examples of global environmental cooperation on policy development.

WHAT WE THINK WE KNOW

Increasingly, environmental policy issues are taking on global dimensions. Such issues as acid rain, ozone depletion, and global warming require multilateral effort and commitment if meaningful policy is to be made. Although each of the cases discussed in Chapter 3 focuses on uniquely local or national problems, all of these issues parallel concerns in other countries. In addition, many environmental concerns such as global warming, acid rain, and genetically modified (GM) foods require cross-boundary cooperation because they have international implications.

Many environmental pollution issues of concern at the regional or national level can affect other countries. Some of these impacts can be direct, for example air pollutants (such as SO_x, NO_x) move from one country to another. Less apparent are indirect environmental impacts that can result from international economic agreements that encourage the relocation of industrial operations to countries where environmental laws may not be as strict. Such indirect environmental impacts were the subject of much debate during negotiation and ultimate ratification of the North America Free Trade Agreement (NAFTA). They are also at the heart of the Trade and Sustainable Development Agenda of the World Trade Organization.

Regional/National Environmental Issues with International Implications

We have discussed the ongoing struggle to come to grips with the issue of chlorinated organic compounds. It is not surprising that advocates on all sides often cite the policies and laws of other countries to support their respective positions. This seemingly regional or national environmental issue has recently been the subject of debate in various multinational settings.

The International Joint Commission (IJC) is a joint U.S.–Canadian agency that oversees and makes recommendations regarding the Great Lakes Water Quality Agreement. In 1992, the IJC, along with the Paris Commission on Land Based Sources of Pollution to the North Atlantic (a 15-nation European body), recommended the elimination of chlorine and chlorine-containing compounds as industrial feedstocks as well as examination of the possibility of reducing or eliminating other uses of these compounds. The IJC based its recommendation on research that supposedly found 168 chlorinated organic compounds in the Great Lakes region and 177 such compounds in humans in North America. IJC made its recommendations in the belief that chlorinated organic compounds should be addressed collectively (Taylor, 1995; Hileman, 1994). The recommendations might seem to have signaled at least some level of international agreement or consensus on the use of chlorinated organic compounds. However, this was not the case.

The following year (1993), Governor John Engler asked the Michigan Environmental Science Board (MESB) to evaluate the scientific basis for

IJC's recommended chlorine phase-out. The Chlorine Panel designated by MESB to conduct the study found that there was "insufficient scientific evidence that short-lived chlorinated compounds produce environmental health threats" (Kirschner, 1994). The panel suggested that current federal and state environmental laws and regulations were "reasonably adequate," but, like IJC, recommended periodic review and better monitoring. IJC, lacking the authority to carry out its proposal, was not able to convince either the U.S. or Canadian government to respond to its findings.

Although not an environmental problem that required joint U.S.–Canadian agreement on the risks associated with the continued use of chlorinated organic compounds, the IJC recommendations show how a national issue can have international implications, in this case a consequence of the transnational location of the Great Lakes, a shared resource. It also demonstrates the ubiquitous tension between scientific uncertainty and economic concerns—factors that led the Canadian and U.S. governments to ignore the IJC's recommendations.

The global conference addressing Persistent Organic Pollutants (POPs) has faced similar obstacles. POPs are a group of chlorinated organic compounds that persist in the environment, bioaccumulate over time through the food web, and pose serious human health and environmental risks. Following the 1992 Earth Summit in Rio de Janeiro, governments agreed in 1997 to formulate a binding global convention to reduce and/or eliminate POPs (Noronha, 1998). In December 2000, the treaty was finalized by 122 countries that will ban or phase out three classes of POPs (Kaiser & Enserink, 2000):

- *Pesticides*—aldrin, chlordane, DDT, dieldrin, endrin, heptachlor, mirex, and toxaphene
- *Industrial chemicals*—hexachlorobenzene and polychlorinated biphenyls (PCBs)
- *Unintended by-products*—dioxins and furans

The majority of these POPs have been "blacklisted" in many countries, including the United States; however, they continue to be used in many other countries throughout the world. There has been considerable debate on the elimination of POPs from industrialized and developing nations alike, and four sessions of the International Negotiating Committee have resulted in general agreements on a number of difficult choices. With each succeeding negotiation session, a greater number of countries decided to participate. Various United Nations (UN) bodies and specialized agencies, international organizations, and nongovernmental organizations (NGOs) participated as well (UNEP, 2000). The treaty calls for the elimination of the specific POPs identified above, with several exceptions. One exception involves the continued limited use of DDT to control vector-borne diseases such as malaria. The treaty calls for dioxins and furans, industrial by-products, to be reduced over time. PCBs used in electrical transformers will be allowed until 2025 as long as leaks from the transformers are prevented through regular maintenance. Agreement was also reached on screening and evaluating other chemicals for inclusion in any forthcoming convention. The treaty was formally signed in May 2001 in Stockholm and will go into effect once fifty countries have ratified it (Kaiser & Enserink, 2000).

In many cases, the negotiations surrounding the POPs convention has been somewhat easier than those concerning other chlorinated organic compounds, as there is little scientific debate about the threat posed by the first two classes of POPs (pesticides and industrial chemicals) to human health and the environment. Instead, negotiations have centered more on developing technical and financial mechanisms to aid developing countries and countries with economies in transition to comply with future requirements.

Changing Priorities

The conventional wisdom suggests that there are marked differences between industrialized countries and developing countries regarding environmental protection and environmental policy. Further, the conventional wisdom supposes that developing countries are so overwhelmed by daily economic problems that they have little time and too few resources to concern themselves with environmental pollution or global environmental problems. Indeed, a great many observers assume that environmental problems will drive a wedge between industrialized countries and the developing nations, as each blames the other for global environmental problems.

Yet in a landmark survey titled *The Health of the Planet* conducted in 1992 by Gallup (Dunlap et al., 1993), most of what is assumed about international perspectives related to the environment is called into question. A comprehensive survey was conducted in twenty-four countries (twelve industrialized and twelve developing). The following are among the survey findings:

- Majorities (twenty-one of twenty-four nations) gave priority to environmental protection even at the risk of slowing economic growth; indeed majorities in seventeen nations (including many of the poorer ones) were willing to pay higher prices to achieve environmental requirements.
- Residents of poor countries rated global problems such as ozone depletion, loss of rain forests, and global warming as seriously as did people in wealthy nations, thereby demonstrating worldwide awareness of global environmental issues.
- In assigning responsibility for global environmental problems, industrialized and developing countries were deemed "both equally responsible."
- As politically sensitive as the question is, residents of developing and industrialized countries were nearly equally likely to assign blame for environmental degradation to "overpopulation."
- Support for providing family planning information and free birth control as a response to population problems was mixed. In developing countries like Uruguay, Brazil, and India, support for this approach exceeded 70 percent. In Japan and Scandinavian countries, support was only 4 percent and 13 percent, respectively. This indicates that developing countries themselves recognize that "overpopulation" is a serious problem; while industrialized countries, where populations are declining or stable, do not share this concern.
- There seemed to be a remarkable consensus on solutions to environmental problems. Citizens around the world give strong support to scientific research and stronger laws regulating industry.

The Gallup study outlined above indicates that many if not all of the people of the world share a concern about the environment. This being the case, it should be possible to conduct environmental policy studies, and work toward agreement on how best to proceed on a global scale. We acknowledge, however, that even with a shared interest in avoiding or responding to environmental problems, there are still substantial obstacles to North–South cooperation, as the cases discussed in the following text demonstrate.

International Environmental Negotiation

The challenge of achieving international environmental policy agreement magnifies all of the difficulties involved in formulating national environmental policy because each country represented will bring all of its views on these issues to the table. A county's representative, or negotiation team, involved in international environmental negotiations, must first be able to reconcile its own internal differences. Taking the United States as an example, a negotiation team will naturally have instructions from the federal government concerning what positions it should take. However, governmental organizations may not agree on a strategy. For example, governmental agencies may have differing views on the issue. Congress will also have its own views that will necessarily reflect regional concerns. Congressional views cannot be disregarded; the U.S. Senate will ultimately have to ratify any agreement reached by the negotiators. Finally, NGOs, grassroots organizations, and private sector interests will also have an opinion on the issue at hand. Assuming the negotiation team can reconcile all of these interests, the challenge then moves to reconciling its position with negotiators from every other country represented—a daunting task (Susskind, 1994). In this arena of environmental diplomacy, several procedural shortcomings have been identified as the primary reason for the failure of global environmental negotiations (Susskind, 1994, p. 7):

- Representation and voting procedures do not guarantee that all countries and interests are treated fairly.
- Scientific and political considerations are not balanced in ways that ensure that the wisest possible agreements will emerge.
- Linkages among environmental concerns and other policy issues are rarely explored or drafted adequately.
- Effective monitoring and enforcement agreements are not implemented.

Addressing these procedural issues may go a long way toward enhancing environmental diplomacy. However, White et al. (1992) argue that international environmental diplomacy is still in its infancy and will require a long period to develop. Additionally, approaching environmental policy on a global scale will not be achieved without "enormous social and political stress."

Policy Study Implications

What we have learned about conducting successful environmental policy studies in the previous chapters of this book is generally applicable to the international environmental policy arena—only the frame of reference is different. As described in Chapter 3, successful environmental policy studies help to

- define the problem in a helpful fashion,
- describe the full range of policy options,
- overcome agency resistance to change,
- provide opportunities to engage stakeholders,
- enhance the legitimacy of particular actions, and
- set resource priorities.

Instead of national government agencies, the audience for international environmental policy studies is made up of sovereign governments, their negotiating teams, and, naturally, the stakeholders involved (NGOs, industry, etc.). Nevertheless, the guidance provided does not necessarily change. The methods for organizing effective international studies discussed in Chapter 4 are no less applicable:

- Selecting and using experts
- Shaping the relationship between sponsors and experts
- Choosing the right institutional auspices
- Reviewing policy study results
- Learning from policy studies
- Setting the policy research agenda

Again, in the international environmental policy context, some of these organizational factors, such as policy learning, may take on special importance. Likewise, institutional auspices may play an enhanced role, for example, when considering studies conducted by national level organizations (USGCRP) versus those conducted by UN chartered agencies (IPCC), both of which will be discussed later in this chapter.

Finally, the choice of a methodological approach to conducting policy studies will again mirror those discussed in Chapter 6:

- Analytical methods
- Rhetorical methods
- Process methods

The methods themselves will not change, although the actors and issues must shift. Keeping the above mentioned factors in mind should help provide a framework for critically analyzing the two international environmental policy efforts that follow.

Two environmental issues that have come to the fore during the last decades of the twentieth century and will carry forward into the twenty-first century are global climate change (global warming) and genetically modified (GM) foods. Policy questions surrounding both involve high degrees of uncertainty and large economic stakes. They also highlight the underlying tension between the developed nations of the North and the developing nations of the South.

GLOBAL WARMING

Swedish chemist Svante Arrhenius (1896) coined the term *greenhouse effect* at the turn of the century. He postulated that increasing concentrations of certain gases such as carbon dioxide in the atmosphere would allow sunlight to penetrate, but retain outgoing infrared radiation, in a manner analogous to a greenhouse. This phenomenon would cause global warming (Arrhenius, 1896).

In the natural functioning of the earth's climate, atmospheric gases—most importantly water vapor and carbon dioxide, and less importantly methane, nitrous oxide, and ozone—trap solar heat reflected from the earth's surface and prevent it from escaping into space. Without this natural greenhouse effect, the earth would be 33°C cooler and could not support life as we know it.

As a result of industrial activity in the past century, however, atmospheric concentrations of greenhouse gases (often referred to as GHGs), and other synthetic gases with similar effect, have increased. In developed and developing countries alike, combustion of fossil fuels, industrial use of synthetic gases, and deforestation have released ever-increasing levels of GHGs into the atmosphere. The scientific community agrees that carbon dioxide levels have risen 20 percent in the past century, and there is also general agreement that the earth's global mean temperature has risen between 0.3°C and 0.6°C in the same period (Abrahamson, 1989). If there is indeed a causal relationship (as it now appears there is) between increased levels of GHGs due to human activity and warming on a global scale, the human community may be faced with changes in the earth's climate and resultant disruptions of our human and natural environment on an unprecedented scale. Yet there is no certainty about the challenge that may face us—we don't know for sure when it will happen, and just how severe it might be (Jain & Urban, 1998).

Policy Options

Given the high levels of scientific uncertainty surrounding this issue, two possible policy options may be considered: delaying any action or taking preventative action.

The argument for delaying action is premised on the idea that prevention and adaptation strategies may in the end be unnecessary, or even inefficient or ineffective due to lack of information. That the costs of these actions would be significant is sufficient justification for standing fast. If the impact of climate change is small or can be easily managed, then efforts to prevent, and plan adaptation to, global warming will provide minimal benefits. If our current understanding of the issue is inadequate to ensure that policies conceived today will be effective in the future, then the cost of present action may not be justified. The argument further supposes that effective and efficient adaptation strategies could be designed if and when climate changes have occurred, thus avoiding prevention strategies that may incur costs without adequate assurance of future benefits.

The argument for preventive action now is premised on the belief that the benefit of avoiding or limiting future costs, damages, and environmental surprises is sufficient justification for action. To pay known costs today may be preferable to incurring unknown costs and far greater environmental damage in the future. Immediate action may limit future damage, whereas delayed action may result only in our inability to reverse or remedy warming in years to come. Our wisest choice may well be to begin now the decades-long process of policy design and implementation, and thus have policies ready in time to meet the situation. If we wait, we may find it impossible to put effective policies in place quickly enough once climatic changes have occurred (Jain & Urban, 1998). Slowly, the international community is moving toward a consensus near the latter position. However, creating policy to solve a problem that probably exists is extremely difficult. Not only is it unknown whether, or to what extent, global warming is taking place, the effects of such warming are still uncertain.

United States Global Change Research Program

In 1990, Congress passed the Global Change Research Act of 1990, which established the United States Global Change Research Program (USGCRP), a 10-year program that was aimed at "understanding and responding to global climate change, including the cumulative effects of human activities and natural processes on the environment to promote discussion toward international protocols in global change research" (NRC, 1999). Title II, cited as the International Cooperation in Global Climate Change Research Act of 1990, sought to foster international and intergovernmental cooperation on the issue of global climate (NRC, 1999). "The central purposes of the USGCRP are

- to observe and document changes in the Earth system;
- to understand why these changes are occurring;
- to improve predictions of future global changes;
- to analyze the environmental, socioeconomic, and health consequences of global change; and
- to support state-of-the-science assessments of global environmental change issues." (NRC, 1999)

These acts provided for oversight by a consortium of National Research Council (NRC) groups, coordinated through the Board on Sustainable Development and its Committee on Global Change Research (CGCR). In its most recent review, the NRC has found that "during the past decade, the USGCRP had realized an impressive array of scientific accomplishments . . . and amendments and adjustments to the Montreal Protocol have benefited from research flowing from the USGCRP" (NRC, 1999). The Montreal Protocol is a comprehensive framework for controlling worldwide emissions of ozone-destroying chlorofluorocarbons (CFCs). However, the NRC also identified several areas that will need to be addressed to improve and increase USGCRP's effectiveness in the future:

- Programmatic focus
- Program balance
- Well-calibrated observations
- Focused scientific strategy

First the NRC review identified a *need for a programmatic focus*, finding that although many USGCRP activities were achieving a great deal of success, many critical global change issues were not receiving adequate focus.

This is partly due to the disaggregation of the effort across numerous governmental agencies and a management framework that has not been as successful as expected. Second, the NRC review identified a *need for program balance*, finding that funding was allocated disproportionately to some USGCRP focus areas over others. Third, the review identified a *need for well-calibrated observations*, noting that high-quality data are a powerful tool for obtaining the necessary insights on global change. Finally, and most emphatically, the review identified a *need for a focused scientific strategy*, noting that "the nation and the world are beginning to make momentous decisions about development, technology, and the environment; at the same time, economic and political factors place severe constraints on budgets for research and infrastructure. A sharp focus on the truly essential investments in research and supporting infrastructure is thus more important than ever" (NRC, 1999).

Interestingly, the majority of the findings of the NRC review discussed here mirror quite closely the shortcomings Rubin, Lave, & Morgan noted with the National Acid Precipitation Assessment Program (NAPAP) (discussed in Chapter 6), particularly the need for integration of efforts and establishing research strategies (Rubin, Lave, & Morgan, 1992). It is yet to be seen what effects the NRC study will have on USGCRP; however, it should be noted that at least to a limited degree, USGCRP activities have affected international policy making by affecting the implementation of the Montreal Protocol (NRC, 1999).

Intergovernmental Panel on Climate Change

Policy work on global warming is by no means limited to national efforts. In 1988, the World Meteorological Organization (WMO) and United Nations Environment Programme (UNEP) established the Intergovernmental Panel on Climate Change (IPCC) to "assess the scientific, technical and socio-economic information relevant for the understanding of the risk of human-induced climate change" (IPCC, 2000). Unlike USGCRP, IPCC does not conduct any new research or monitor climate change–related data, but instead bases its assessments on published and peer reviewed scientific literature. IPCC consists of working groups that assess the scientific aspects of the climate system and climate change, the vulnerability of socioeconomic and natural systems to climate change, strategies for adaptation to climate change as well as options for limiting greenhouse gas emissions, and other ways of mitigating climate change. An IPCC task force also oversees the

National Greenhouse Gas Inventories Programme that develops guidelines and methodologies for calculating greenhouse gas emissions and removals. The working groups have published a number of policy documents, including five-year assessment reports, as well as reports concerning emissions scenarios, economic impacts of climate change, mitigation strategies, and land use.

The IPCC First Assessment Report, completed in 1990, played an important role in establishing the Intergovernmental Negotiation Committee for the UN Framework Convention on Climate Change (UNFCCC) by the UN General Assembly and played a critical role in the UN-sponsored Earth Summit in Rio in 1992. In 1992 at the Earth Summit in Rio, the United States signed a treaty that established voluntary goals for returning to 1990 levels of GHG emissions by the year 2000. Because progress toward these voluntary goals was less than satisfactory, negotiations got underway to strengthen the global warming treaty signed by President Bush in 1992. The result was the Kyoto Protocol, signed in 1997.

Kyoto Conference

The Kyoto Conference (or the third Conference of parties to the UN-FCCC), held in Kyoto, Japan, in December 1997, was an international conference with the goal of creating policies that would reduce or at least limit the emission of GHGs worldwide to mitigate, or at least slow, global warming and its potential effects. However, the feeling is that a reduction in anthropogenic sources of GHGs can only help the environment. On the other hand, no nation wants to be targeted for fossil fuel reductions, for fear of adverse economic effects. Thus the task of the policy makers at the Kyoto Conference was immense.

Perhaps the most intractable problem encountered during the conference was defining the contribution that developing countries, known as the Group of 77 (G-77), should make toward GHG reduction. The view of most developing countries (and the policy contained in the 1992 Climate Change Convention) is that developed countries are responsible for the greater percentage of GHGs produced to the present day and thus should be the ones to cut back first. Developed countries are concerned that developing countries, which are growing rapidly, will soon become the major GHG producers and thus should be responsible for reducing their emissions as well. The G-77 "acquiesced to a U.S. proposal that would allow American companies to receive credit against pollution-cutting targets by making deals to help clean up foreign factories" (Witter, 1997). This "clean development mechanism" helped pave the way for agreement at the Kyoto Conference.

On December 11, 1997, thirty-eight developed countries agreed to reduce worldwide emissions of six GHGs, amending the Climate Change Treaty by adding the Kyoto Protocol. The GHGs targeted are carbon dioxide, methane, nitrous oxide, hydrofluorocarbons, perfluorocarbons, and sulfur hexafluoride. Each developed country was placed in one of eight groups ranging from a reduction of 8 percent to an increase of 10 percent. The reduction of GHG emissions of all developed nations is expected to total 5.2 percent between 2008 and 2012. "Among the key industrial players, the United States is required to reduce emissions by 7 percent, the European Union by 8 percent, and Japan by 6 percent" (Oshima & Murakami, 1997). The reductions might not all be actual reductions. Countries may be permitted to subtract the amount of GHGs absorbed by forests within their borders (Oshima & Murakami, 1997), although the method for doing this has still not been determined.

The Kyoto Protocol provides for flexible mechanisms for achieving these reductions. Countries with binding greenhouse gas emissions reduction targets can, for example, use "emissions trading" to meet their commitments, although the specific rules for such trading have not been set. Under one proposed emissions trading scenario, countries, and their authorized private entities, would be allowed to purchase emissions allowances from each other. For example, a country whose cost of controlling GHG emissions is lower than another country's may opt to sell a portion of its emissions allowance to the country where costs of reduction are higher. In theory, the net effect on global GHG reduction would be the same except that the target reduction would be reached at a lower total cost (U.S. EPA, 1999a). Although this mechanism appears simple on the surface, monitoring, enforcement, and liability issues present significant and complex obstacles to its realization (Baron, 1999; OECD, 1999).

To encourage developed nations to help developing nations, a "clean development mechanism" (CDM) was established by which developed countries will be given emission reduction credits for providing assistance to developing countries in their efforts to reduce GHG emissions. A CDM might, for example, involve a company from an industrialized country (presumably having a binding GHG reduction target) that would help design and build a highly efficient plant in a developing country in place of a previously planned, less efficient plant. The difference in GHG reductions between the planned plant and the efficient plant would result in certified emissions reductions (CEMs) that could be shared by the developing nation and the company from the industrialized nation. The developing nation could opt to save or sell any resulting CEMs while the company in the industrialized country could use the CEMs to meet its own GHG reduction commitments (U.S. EPA, 1999b). In principal, a CDM should result in the same net global reduction in GHGs while at the same time promoting sustainable development, encouraging countries to meet environmental goals, and spurring technology transfer and investment. However, as with emissions trading, hurdles to implementing CDMs include criteria for project selection, standards for accreditation of certifiers, and liability for noncompliance (Toman & Cazorla, 1998).

Several other issues still need to be worked out, including the benchmark year from which each of the six GHGs will be reduced. Some GHGs will be reduced from 1990 levels, whereas others will be reduced from 1995 levels. Although the Kyoto Conference took an important step toward addressing the issue of global warming, the benefit to the environment and the economic impact of the conference have yet to be determined. A major potential stumbling block for the United States is ratification in the Senate, where U.S. negotiators have indicated that ratification of the treaty hinges on the "meaningful participation" of developing nations (Corliss, 2000), though such participation has yet to be defined.

Interrelationship of National and International Efforts and the Role of Technology

In many ways, the "successful" negotiations resulting in the Kyoto Protocol were based on policy efforts that incorporated many of the positive attributes we have discussed in previous chapters. Although it is quite difficult to discuss the uses of policy studies (Chapter 3) without an in-depth analysis of the policy studies prepared, judging from the outcome of the Kyoto Conference, it is possible that some of the policy studies prepared aided the parties in reaching agreement on many contentious issues by defining the issue in a helpful manner, overcoming resistance to change, and providing opportunities for engaging stakeholders. Somewhat more amenable to discussion is the application of the organizational concepts discussed in Chapter 4.

The USGCRP had an extremely credible sponsor/oversight organization—the NRC. Next, the umbrella nature of the endeavor (climate change research) allowed experts with a wide range of backgrounds to study and address the global climate change issue. Periodic review and the opportunity to refocus research and policy efforts have also enhanced the credibility and impact of its products. Finally, the structure of the USGCRP, in conjunction with the CGCR, has provided the opportunity to set an appropriate and effective research policy agenda.

The policy efforts of the IPCC pick up where the USGCRP leaves off. In effect, the IPCC integrates USGCRP reports, along with credible scientific reports from around the world, in conducting its policy studies and formulating policy options. In a sense, IPCC uses analytical methods to select and include credible international scientific and policy studies in its own policy studies. However, when preparing its own analyses and formulating policy options, rhetorical and process methods will come into play. IPCC, formed under the auspices of UNEP, gains a large measure of credibility due to its UN affiliation. One other crucial organizational aspect, which may have lent support and credibility to its resulting policy studies and assessments, is that, in the broadest possible sense, it involved various stakeholder groups. In this case, the stakeholder groups are the nations themselves. The involvement, other than the typical negotiations that precede any international agreement, is the synthesis of scientific reports and policy studies from nations around the world, one of the uses of successful environmental policy studies previously discussed. Although the IPCC does not have the direct authority to cause scientific studies to be carried out on its behalf on specific topics, it does possess an indirect authority by virtue of the working groups and task forces it forms and the specific topics they are charged to address. Given the uncertainties surrounding the global climate change debate, it is interesting to speculate on whether the UNFCCC would have been formed or the topic of global climate change even addressed at the Earth Summit in Rio in 1992 absent the policy studies and assessments conducted by the IPCC.

In addition to many national and international efforts to address global climate change, one cannot ignore the possibility of technological alternatives that may ameliorate the build-up of GHGs. One such approach deals with capturing carbon dioxide resulting from fossil fuel combustion in power plants and sequestering it for centuries in deep aquifers, the ocean, or geologic formations (Allenby, 2000). The main questions regarding these emerging approaches usually are: Do the technologies exist and are they economically feasible?

According to some studies (Socolow, 1997), if carbon sequestration is implemented early in the design stage of the project, carbon sequestration systems are technologically and economically feasible. One example cited is the successful implementation of such an approach by Norway's state-owned petroleum company, Statoil. Statoil is currently sequestering the carbon dioxide content of the natural gas it is extracting from a field off the coast of Norway back into an aquifer approximately 1000 meters below the seabed (Allenby, 2000). From an economic point of view, the cost of this system was preferable to paying the $55 per ton tax that would be levied if carbon dioxide were vented to the atmosphere (Allenby, 2000).

Long-term unintended environmental impacts are always of concern when implementing new technologies, such as carbon sequestration. Further development of technologies to minimize the release of GHGs to the environment, development of alternatives such as hydrogen technologies, conservation, along with national and international cooperation in reducing GHGs would be needed to affect in a meaningful way this challenging potential problem.

The issue of global climate change is far from resolved. Agreements hammered out in Kyoto are still being addressed as negotiators try to agree on permissible methods of achieving GHG emissions limitations and the degree to which new technologies and approaches can be employed to achieve results. Invariably, environmental policy studies will provide the primary mechanism for making this critical information available to the negotiating parties. Employing suggestions provided in previous chapters of this book could ensure that the information contained in environmental policy studies reaches policy makers in a form that can be assimilated, understood, and used as a basis for decision making on this critical environmental issue.

GENETICALLY MODIFIED FOODS

Although recent news coverage has focused on trade and human health–related issues, environmental issues are playing an increasingly large role in the ongoing debate surrounding genetically modified (GM) food. As with the global warming debate, the science surrounding the environmental impacts of the use and continued development of GM foods is highly uncertain. This creates a difficult set of circumstances for making policy.

Transgenic Crops

GM foods per se are not "new," as some form of "genetic modification" has been carried out for centuries. Plant breeding involves crossbreeding a crop with another plant from the same or similar species possessing a desired characteristic. Usually, such crossbreeding would produce a range of hybrids and only the hybrid containing all of the desired characteristics would ultimately be selected for cultivation. Often, this process was carried out over several generations to obtain the desired mix of characteristics.

Plant breeding, however, is limited by the fact that only species relatively close to one another can be crossbred and the process can take months or years to achieve the desired end product. Advances in genetic engineering now allow scientists to take a gene responsible for a desired trait from any plant, animal, insect, bacterium, virus, or other living organism, and through gene-splicing or similar procedures, incorporate the desired gene into the target plant, resulting in so-called transgenic plants or crops. The advantage of these processes over traditional plant breeding is that traits can be more accurately targeted and results can be more quickly obtained. However, the risk of achieving unexpected and potentially deleterious results is higher (Yoon, 1999b).

Currently, when GM foods are debated, it is not the fact that the food has been genetically altered that is the issue. Instead, it is the reality that a modern biotechnology process has been used to bring about the desired alteration and that the alteration may generate surprising (and dangerous) impacts. Thus the term *GM foods* is used not to refer to crops produced by traditional plant breeding, but to those produced by modern gene-splicing technology (Spencer, 1999).

In 1992, transgenic crops first began to be considered for approval by the U.S. Food and Drug Administration (FDA), the U.S. agency ultimately responsible for reviewing and approving GM foods. The FDA approved the widespread planting of GM tomatoes for the first time in 1994. Since that time, over thirty different GM crops have been approved by the FDA, including corn, soybeans, potatoes, and cotton. Currently, approximately 25 percent of the acreage cultivated with corn consists of GM corn varieties. Similarly, about 38 percent of soybean-cultivated acreage and 50 percent of cotton-cultivated acreage is planted with GM varieties of these crops. In sum, about 60 million hectares (144 million acres) in the United States are cultivated with some form of GM crops, and over 70 percent of food in U.S. grocery stores may include some GM food product (Agence France-

Presse, 1999; Barboza, 2000a; Brown, Renner, & Halweil, 2000). U.S. officials estimate that by 2004 nearly all U.S. agricultural exports will consist of GM foods or be combined with GM bulk commodities (Reuters, 1999).

Transgenic crops include seeds and plants that have been genetically altered to produce desirable "input" characteristics such as larger crops and increased survivability in the face of adversity—resistance to drought conditions, resistance to pests, and so forth. One example of an "input" transgenic crop is a strain of cotton that has been genetically modified to withstand exposure to Roundup, a popular herbicide (Myerson, 1998). Another such crop is called "Bt corn" because it carries a gene derived from the *Bacillus thuringiensis* bacterium. The gene produces the Bt toxin that kills corn-boring pests that try to eat the corn crop (Yoon, 1999a).

Other transgenic crops result from plants and seeds that have been altered to produce desirable "output" characteristics resulting, for example, in high-oil corn designed for fattening livestock (Brown, Renner, & Halweil, 1999). Another example of an "output" transgenic crop is rice that has been genetically engineered to include three genes that produce "Golden Rice," rich in beta carotene, the source of vitamin A. Two biotechnology companies have contacted about eighty developing countries in Africa, Asia, and Latin America to donate Golden Rice seeds to them. According to Phillips, they have welcomed receiving these seeds, which they hope will help prevent blindness—a human health effect of vitamin A deficiency (Phillips, 2000).

Policy Issues

Several factors combine to put GM foods into the international environmental spotlight. First, because the widespread planting and use of GM foods may have unintended environmental consequences, they may ultimately affect ecosystems on a global scale by creating various resistant strains of organisms and possibly by causing species extinction altogether (Rissler & Mellon, 1996). Second, because GM foods constitute a large and growing percentage of U.S. agricultural exports, concerns voiced in other countries as to the ultimate human health effects of GM foods can and have impacted international trade in these commodities, thus elevating the issue of GM foods to the international arena.

The ability to splice genes and create novel crop strains with enhanced input and output characteristics raises the question of whether this technology should be used at all (Rissler & Mellon, 1996). Those opposed to the continued development, planting, and consumption of GM foods argue three main policy points: First, that genetic manipulation constitutes an act against nature; second, that the food produced by GM means is dangerous to human health; and third, that the cultivation of GM food damages the environment (Hoge, 1999).

Some claim that GM foods represent an act against nature. Supporters of transgenic techniques argue that GM foods are no different from foods produced by more traditional plant breeding methods, and that only the process is different (Spencer, 1999). However, it is precisely the process that calls GM foods into question. Many argue that the introduction of genes from different species, and possibly distantly related plants or completely unrelated organisms, pose unknown and thus unacceptable risks to human health and the environment.

Probably the most vocal resistance to GM foods has come from Europe where many say that GM foods, dubbed "Frankenfoods," pose potential human health effects and that eating GM foods may alter human genes, thus constituting an unacceptable health risk. Commentators have suggested that such widespread distrust of GM foods has its roots in the recent (1996) outbreak of mad cow disease in Great Britain, and the incident of dioxin-contaminated chicken in Belgium (Cohen, 1999; Hoge, 1999). Hoge speculates that such distrust also exists because, "[t]here is no government agency in Europe with the regulatory rigor of the U.S. Food and Drug Administration to build consumer confidence, and government approval can arouse suspicion as much as it can provide reassurance" (Hoge, 1999). Supporters counter that GM foods have been consumed for years in the United States with no incidents of negative human health effects. Spencer further argues that the risks posed by GM foods are no different from those posed by foods that have been genetically modified by the more traditional method of plant breeding. As an example, Spencer cites the Lenape potato, a strain of potato developed through traditional plant breeding techniques that produced better chips. However, the crossbreeding producing the Lenape potato resulted in elevated levels of toxic glycoalkaloids in the potato. Because of this problem, the Lenape potato was removed from the market in the 1970s. This example, according to Spencer (1999), illustrates the fact that unintended consequences are just as likely in crop strains developed by traditional cross-breeding methods as with biotechnologically produced foods. But, just because such consequences are "as likely" does not necessarily mean that GM foods are safe to either human health or the environment. This debate has dominated the landscape of GM foods.

Recently, the debate concerning GM foods has come to include potential irreversible harm to the ecosystem. A laboratory study conducted by researchers from Cornell University suggests that Bt corn (discussed previously) produces an airborne pollen that can kill monarch butterflies that breed in regions of the United States where corn is the predominant crop (Yoon, 1999a). Other environmental consequences include the possibility that resistance to Bt may evolve more quickly as Bt corn gains greater acceptance and widespread planting (Yoon, 1999b). There is also a possibility that foreign genes incorporated into crops will escape to "wild" varieties by interbreeding. This could potentially result in a "superweed" endowed with the same herbicide-resistant qualities as the GM variety. Although GM corn, soybeans, and cotton do not pose such a risk in this country as there are no plants with which they can interbreed, GM rice, beets, canola, sunflowers, cranberries, and strawberries pose such a potential risk. Once again, supporters counter this concern that these are the same risks posed by plants modified by traditional plant breeding methods. Additionally, the benefits gained from using GM crops, such as the use of lower quantities of environmentally friendly herbicides such as Roundup, and eliminating the need, in the case of Bt corn, for pesticides, may be less damaging to the monarch butterfly and insect diversity in general (Yoon, 1999b). More recent studies further complicate the cost–benefit and risk–benefit analysis of GM foods. For example, a research team from the University of Illinois found that pollen from the Mon 810 variety of Bt corn did not appear to harm swallowtail butterflies either in the lab or in the field. However, another strain, Bt corn "176," was toxic to swallowtail butterflies in the laboratory. The Cornell study cited above used yet a third variety of Bt corn called "Bt 11" (Yoon, 2000b). There may exist a Bt variety that achieves the objective of toxicity toward corn boring pests but at the same time is safe to the rest of the ecosystem. But which one is it?

The issue apparently does not concern only various species of butterflies. A private grass seed company involved in developing GM grass varieties discovered that pollen can travel over 1,000 feet, possibly as far as 3,000 feet, and can thus cross-fertilize with different strains of grass—creating new, unintended, genetically modified breeds. However, individuals from a group calling itself the Anarchist Golfing Association destroyed plots of genetically modified grass at the seed company, effectively halting any further research of the possible dangers posed by new GM grass varieties (Barboza, 2000b).

Scientific research tends to demonstrate that the environmental risks posed by transgenic crops/GM foods are not generic. GM crops do not share one common enhanced trait such as aggressive growth or pest resistance. The risks posed by such crops may ultimately depend on a combination of novel characteristics. Many GM crops will not be harmful and indeed will confer some benefit. But at the same time, the overall risk of environmental harm will rise with the number and variety of crops developed and released (Rissler & Mellon, 1996).

National Policy

Nationally, an increased awareness of the potential environmental dangers posed by the increased cultivation and production of GM foods has resulted in some policy changes. In 1999, the FDA announced that it was reviewing its procedures for approving GM foods to ensure that environmental as well as other concerns raised are being adequately addressed (Feder, 1999). In addition, in January 2000, the U.S. EPA announced new regulations targeted to reduce risks posed by Bt corn. The regulations direct biotech seed companies to ask farmers to voluntarily plant unmodified corn around the edges of Bt cornfields, thus creating a buffer zone to protect butterflies. Additionally, farmers would be required to plant at least 20 percent non-Bt corn; however, there is no requirement that the non-Bt corn be planted in a buffer zone (Yoon, 2000a). Finally, in July 2000, the National Academy of Sciences (NAS) joined six other foreign academies of science to urge the increased development and use of biotechnology in developing nations to address hunger and poverty. The report calls for a regulatory system to be put in place in every country to monitor human health risks from GM plants and to research human health and environmental risks posed by GM plants (Yoon, 2000c).

However, these moves, even coupled with scientific reports bolstering claims of the safety of GM foods, have not generated the degree of public confidence in GM foods that might have been expected. There are several possible explanations. For one, there has been no formal, credible policy study of GM foods. Recent reports have disclosed considerable disagreement within the FDA in the early 1990s as to the degree to which new GM foods should be regulated. One document written by an FDA scientist accused the FDA of "siding with industry" and not addressing the fact that "there is no data that addresses the relative magnitude of risk" posed by GM foods (Burros, 1999). Public confidence of the NAS was also shaken when, in August 1999, a scientist directing a study on genetically engineered crops for the NAS violated ethical rules by not disclosing any conflicts with industries affected by the academy's studies. The scientist announced a few days before leaving that he was going to work for the Biotechnology Industry Organization, a trade association in Washington, D.C., that represents some eight hundred biotechnology companies (Petersen, 1999). The NAS study was to have been one of the first comprehensive efforts to examine the risks and benefits posed by GM foods.

Unlike the studies conducted by the USGCRP and IPCC concerning global climate change (discussed earlier), policy studies and research surrounding human health and environmental risks posed by GM foods do not appear to possess many of the attributes of successful policy studies discussed in previous chapters. The loss of credibility, no matter how good the science, may have doomed the FDA and NAS efforts. Indeed, many are calling the NAS's recent announcement in support of biotechnology as "merely an attempt by scientists to gain public support for a technology that is becoming increasingly unpopular" (Yoon, 2000c).

International Attention

Although driven by trade, not environmental, concerns, the GM food issue entered the international arena in the late 1990s. On January 29, 2000, over 130 nations agreed to the Cartagena Protocol on Biosafety (Biosafety Protocol), that would set up an international framework for dealing with trade issues surrounding GM foods (Pollack, 2000b). The Biosafety Protocol was an outgrowth of the 1992 Convention on Biological Diversity. Because the U.S. Senate never ratified this convention, the United States, arguably the country that would be most affected by the protocol, had no vote on the Biosafety Protocol and was forced to rely on its allies to vote for provisions backed by the United States. The United States and five other grain producing and exporting countries had blocked previous attempts at a treaty, arguing that requirements to obtain permission in advance before exporting GM grain to other countries would result in unacceptable trade barriers to GM foods, absent clear scientific evidence of harm (Pollack, 2000a).

Nevertheless, even without a vote, nearly all of the provisions sought by the United States were agreed to in the Cartagena Protocol. First, GM foods would not have to be segregated and labeled during international shipment. Instead, they would only have to be labeled that they might contain genetically modified organisms. Second, exporters would have to obtain permission in advance before the first shipment of "living modified organisms" intended for release into the environment, such as seeds, microbes, and fish. However, permission would not have to be sought for agricultural products intended for consumption and further processing such as grain (Pollack, 2000b). Although produced as a trade agreement, the Protocol, according to Pollack, is mainly concerned with protecting the environment. It represents "perhaps the strongest formulation of the 'precautionary principle' . . . [that] states that a nation can take action to protect itself—in this case by barring import of a genetically modified organism—even if there is a lack of scientific certainty that it would be dangerous" (Pollack, 2000b). Delegates touted the Protocol as a rare success in balancing environmental protection with free trade issues (Pollack, 2000b).

Although the Biosafety Protocol represents a major international agreement concerning GM foods, several environmental policy issues remain that will need to be addressed in the future. The GM foods debate has largely centered on agricultural products. Cattle and other livestock have already been fed genetically modified grain for years but industry does not consider meat from these animals to constitute GM foods (Knox, 2000). However, scientists are currently developing strains of genetically engineered chickens, altered to make them resistant to poultry parasites, and cloning cattle to produce high-grade beef (AP, 2000a,b). Beef treated with hormones has already resulted in trade retaliation between the United States and European countries. As genetic modification becomes more prevalent in animals, new international environmental issues will likely arise.

GM seed producing companies have also begun to develop sterile seeds. These GM seeds would force farmers to buy seeds annually rather than retain seeds from a previous year's crop. Opponents argue that this development would constitute an undue strain on farmers, particularly those in developing countries, where farmers traditionally rely on seeds generated from a previous year's crop. Although at least one major manufacturer of GM seeds in the United States had announced it will not market such seeds, these seeds actually may represent one way of controlling unanticipated environmental consequences from GM seeds. By linking the sterility characteristic to other modified traits, these seeds would ensure that if the genes "jumped" to wild varieties of plants in the environment, the modification would only survive one season, as any resulting "weeds" would also be sterile. In any case, such a development is nearly a decade in the future, but will ultimately need to be addressed (Feder, 1999).

Finally, the issue of crops and livestock that have been genetically engineered to enhance nutrition or produce pharmaceuticals will become increasingly prevalent in the years to come. Up to now, most crop seeds have been genetically modified to resist pests and withstand harsh climate conditions. More recently, newer GM crops have been genetically engineered to enhance the nutritional value of foods, as in the example of Golden Rice. With respect to animals, goat embryos have been modified with synthetic human DNA to raise goats that produce pharmaceuticals in their milk. As could be expected, pharmaceuticals produced by GM animals raise human health concerns, such as the possibility of the unintended introduction of viruses and other infections in the pharmaceuticals produced. In spite of these concerns, developers expect the FDA to approve marketing of pharmaceuticals produced by GM animals within two years (Knox, 2000).

As the world's population continues to increase and arable land decreases, the world will face an increasing need for new varieties of crops. The Biosafety Protocol, although broadly addressing issues surrounding GM foods, says nothing about pharmaceuticals produced by GM animals or plants (Pollack, 2000b). The Biosafety Protocol thus represents an important first step in reaching global consensus in addressing these complex environmental issues. However, it will not replace the need for credible, national and international environmental policy studies, based on scientific data, that address the human health and environmental risks and benefits associated with GM foods.

Designing credible policy studies will be challenging. The problems/issues will have to be carefully defined. Once defined, all policy options will have to be discussed and elaborated upon. Clearly, there are differing opinions as to what constitutes GM foods. Defining the problem/issue in a helpful fashion could move the debate beyond these initial, definitional stumbling blocks. Organizational factors such as selecting credible experts who bring a range of backgrounds to the issue, stakeholder involvement, and possibly multilateral task forces may provide the necessary ingredients. Invariably, due to the contentious nature of this issue, a rhetorical or process approach will most likely need to be adopted when conducting the study. Only by including stakeholders in the policy analysis process will studies achieve the level of credibility required to address the criticism that has been leveled at GM foods.

CONCLUDING REMARKS

Clark (1995) argues that one of the primary obstacles to conducting environmental policy analysis on a global scale is the quality of data or "environmental intelligence" available. For example, analysts may take for granted that all major countries with market economies can provide credible information concerning such factors as income, employment, and trade, as well as environmental factors such as the types and scales of pollution. Without credible and more in-depth information, however, discussion of possible reforms of global environmental policy will be largely symbolic.

In spite of the lack of credible environmental information (as discussed earlier) and a perceived unwillingness to act on a global scale, there are several policy concepts that may ultimately enhance this effort. First, on a national and international scale, efforts should probably be directed toward a "cross-media" approach. Too often environmental policy studies focus on pollution in a single medium such as air or water, while disregarding the interactions among them. It would probably be prudent to conduct comprehensive multi- and cross-media environmental analysis to achieve meaningful global perspectives.

Second, economic incentives should be studied as a policy instrument to enhance the efficacy of global environmental action. A case in point would be the issue of global warming. Developing countries frequently engage in activities to enhance their development while at the same time increasing carbon dioxide levels in the atmosphere. Although efforts to reduce carbon dioxide emissions in developed countries may be practical, economic incentives may hold the key to persuading some counties to forgo practices that enhance carbon dioxide emissions without compromising their efforts at development.

Finally, movement toward sustainable development practices—"development that meets the needs of the present without compromising the ability of future generations to meet their own needs" (Parson & Clark, 1993) may prove to be the most prudent. Many of the ongoing criticisms of the idea of sustainable development, including the difficulty of defining the level of sustainability to aim for and decisions about who ultimately decides or sets this level, still need to be resolved.

Problems surrounding international environmental policy development are indeed substantial. Environmental issues, which at first appear national, may indeed affect other counties, as discussed concerning pollution of the Great Lakes by chlorinated organics. Contrary to the conventional wisdom, a majority of the world's population favors efforts to protect and preserve the environment. But reaching global environmental consensus has been a difficult and painful process. Some degree of success was achieved by the signing of the Kyoto Protocol in 1997, which established national GHG emissions limitations. However, implementation of the protocol has proven to be problematic. The debate concerning GM foods continues to rage. Although an international trade agreement was reached concerning GM foods, the debate concerning their ultimate safety and the potential for irreversible environmental and ecological harm persists. Whether in the national or the international arena, environmental policy studies represent the primary mechanism available for providing the information that policy and decision makers will need to craft effective policy. Applying the strategies presented in this book concerning the uses and organization of environmental policy studies and the approaches to conducting them should help to ensure the availability of more useful and effective policy studies.

Appendix A—National Academy of Sciences National Research Council Report Review Guidelines

The material reproduced here comes from a pamphlet published by the National Academy of Sciences (NAS). A copy of the pamphlet, which contains guidelines outlining the review procedures and the reviewers' responsibilities, accompanies National Resources Council (NRC) reports that have entered the review process.

Any NRC or Institute of Medicine (IOM) report (including meeting summaries, signed papers, letter reports, or other study products) must be reviewed by a diverse group of experts other than its authors before it may be released outside the institution. This independent, rigorous review is a hallmark that distinguishes the NRC/IOM from many other organizations offering scientific and technical advice on issues of national importance.

Purpose. The purpose of review is to assist the authors in making their report as accurate and effective as possible and to ensure that they and the NRC/IOM are creditably represented by the report published in both their names. Review not only fulfills the institutional obligation to exercise oversight, but also provides the authors with preliminary reactions from a diverse group of experts and, as a result, enhances the clarity, cogency, and credibility of the final document. Reviewers are asked to consider whether in their judgment the evidence and arguments presented are sound and the report is fully responsive to the study charge, *not* whether they concur with the findings.

Process. The report review process is overseen by the Report Review Committee (RRC), made up of approximately thirty members of the NAS, National Academy of Engineering, and IOM. The process is managed by the commission, board, or office responsible for institutional oversight of the project. This NRC/IOM administrative unit, in consultation with the RRC, appoints a group of independent reviewers with diverse perspectives on key issues considered in the report. A draft report is sent to reviewers only after all authors have indicated that they are satisfied with its form and content. Reviewers receive the complete report (including front matter, preface, executive summary, and all appendices), along with the statement of task and this brochure. Reviewers are asked to provide written comments on any and all aspects of the draft report, but to pay particular attention to the review criteria set forth in the final section of this brochure. The authors are expected to consider all review comments and to provide written responses, which are evaluated by the monitor (appointed by the RRC) and/or review coordinator (appointed by the NRC/IOM administrative unit). A report may not be released to the sponsors or the public, nor may its findings be disclosed, until after the review process has been satisfactorily completed and all authors have approved the revised draft.

Confidentiality and Anonymity. To encourage reviewers to express their views freely, the review comments are treated as confidential documents and are given to the authors of the report with identifiers removed. After submitting their comments, reviewers are asked to return or destroy the draft manuscript and to refrain from disclosing their comments or the contents of the draft. The names and affiliations of participants in the review will be made public when the report is released (usually by acknowledgment in the printed report), but their comments remain confidential. Even after release of the report, reviewers should not divulge their comments or any changes made to the draft manuscript. These restrictions are imperative in safeguarding the integrity of the institutional review process.

Supporting Evidence. The rationale for any findings, conclusions, and recommendations should be fully explained in the report. This explanation might include references to the literature, analysis of data, or a description of the pros and cons of the range of alternatives and the reasons for preferring a particular option. Failure to document conclusions and recommendations adequately is the most common shortcoming of draft reports. Of particular concern are recommendations calling for organizational changes or budgetary increases within government agencies. In general, such recommendations should be avoided unless specifically called for in the study charge.

Executive Summary. Every major report should have a brief executive summary (no more than 5,000 words) that identifies the study charge and provides a synopsis of the key findings. This summary should be easily comprehensible to nonexperts. While the executive summary should accurately reflect the text of the report, it need not include all of the conclusions and recommendations.

Consensus and Dissent. NRC/IOM committees strive for consensus, but on rare occasions—despite extensive deliberations—one or more committee members may not concur with the views of the majority. Matters of disagreement should be addressed forthrightly in the report. As a final recourse, a committee member may choose to prepare a brief dissent (no more than 5,000 words) succinctly describing the issues of contention and the arguments in support of the minority view. This statement should be included as an appendix to the draft report, with reference to it in the introductory text and Table of Contents. A dissent may not address issues outside the study charge, misrepresent the majority's views, or contain other inaccuracies. Any questions regarding the appropriateness of material included in a dissent shall be referred to the RRC chair. Although reviewers' comments on the statement are given to its author for consideration, no formal written response is required.

Review Criteria. NRC/IOM reports cover a broad range of topics and appear in a variety of different forms. Although no rigid set of criteria is likely to be applicable to all reports, reviewers may find the following questions useful in formulating their comments. (A separate set of criteria is used for "letter reports" and other abbreviated documents.)

1. Is the charge clearly described in the report? Are all aspects of the charge fully addressed? Do the authors go beyond their charge or their expertise?
2. Are the conclusions and recommendations adequately supported by evidence, analysis, and argument? Are uncertainties or incompleteness in the evidence explicitly recognized? If any recommendations are based on value judgments or the collective opinions of the authors, is this acknowledged and are adequate reasons given for reaching those judgments? If the report is based on a workshop, are findings and conclusions attributed to either an individual or NRC committee?
3. Are the data and analyses handled competently? Are statistical methods applied appropriately?
4. Are sensitive policy issues treated with proper care? For example, if the report contains recommendations pertaining to the reorganization of an agency or the creation of a new institutional entity, are the advantages and disadvantages of alternative options, including the status quo, considered?

5. Are the report's exposition and organization effective? Is the title appropriate?

6. Is the report fair? Is its tone impartial and devoid of special pleading?

7. Does the executive summary concisely and accurately describe the key findings and recommendations? Is it consistent with other sections of the report?

8. Are signed papers or appendices, if any, relevant to the charge? If the report relies on signed papers to support consensus findings or recommendations, do the papers meet criterion 3 above?

9. What other significant improvements, if any, might be made in the report?

In providing comments, reviewers are encouraged to distinguish issues they consider to be of general/major concern from other, less significant points.

NATIONAL REVIEW COMMITTEE
December 1997

Acronyms

AARC	Alternative Agricultural Research and Commercialization Program (USDA)
ACF	Advocacy Coalition Framework
AFL-CIO	American Federation of Labor and Congress of Industrial Organizations
AP	Associated Press
ARS	Agricultural Research Service (USDA)
BLM	Bureau of Land Management (DOI)
BOTEHH/CLS	Board on Toxicology and Environmental Health Hazards/Committee on Life Sciences (NRC)
CAA	Clean Air Act
CAST	Council on Agricultural Sciences and Technology
CDM	Clean Development Mechanism
CEMs	Certified Emissions Reductions
CERCLA	Comprehensive Environmental Response, Compensation, and Liability Act
CFCs	Chlorofluorocarbons
CGCR	Committee on Global Change Research (NRC)
CO	Carbon monoxide
DDT	1,1,1-trichloro-2,2-bis (p-chloriphenyl)-ethane
DOE	Department of Energy
DOI	Department of the Interior
EMAP	Environmental Monitoring Assessment Program (EPA)
EPA	United States Environmental Protection Agency
ESA	Endangered Species Act
FDA	Food and Drug Administration
FDCA	Food, Drug, and Cosmetic Act
FFERDC	Federal Facilities Environmental Restoration Dialogue Committee (EPA)
FIFRA	Federal Insecticide, Fungicide, and Rodenticide Act
FWS	Fish and Wildlife Service (DOI)

G-77	Group of 77 (nations)
GAO	General Accounting Office
GHGs	Greenhouse Gases
GM	Genetically Modified
IJC	International Joint Committee
IOM	Institute of Medicine
IPCC	Intergovernmental Panel on Climate Change
ISC	Interagency Scientific Committee to Address the Conservation of the Northern Spotted Owl
LP	Linear Program
MESB	Michigan Environmental Science Board
NAE	National Academy of Engineering
NAFTA	North America Free Trade Agreement
NAPAP	National Acid Precipitation Assessment Program
NAS	National Academy of Sciences
NEPA	National Environmental Policy Act
NGO	Nongovernmental Organization
NIMBY	"Not in my backyard"
NO_x	Nitric Oxides
NPS	National Park Service (DOI)
NRC	National Research Council (NAS)
NRDC	Natural Resources Defense Council
NSF	National Science Foundation
NWC	Nuclear Weapons Complex
OECD	Organization for Economic Cooperation and Development
OMB	Office of Management and Budget (White House)
OR	Operations Research
OTA	Office of Technology Assessment (US Congress)
PCBs	Polychlorinated biphenyls
P.L.	Public Law
POPs	Persistent Organic Pollutants
RFP	Request for Proposal
RRC	Report Review Committee (NAS/NRC)
RRRSC	Relative Risk Reduction Strategies Committee (EPA/SAB)
SAB	Science Advisory Board (EPA)
SO_x	Sulfur Oxides
SSAB	Site Specific Advisory Board

Task Force	The New Farm and Forest Products Task Force (USDA)
UN	United Nations
UNEP	United Nations Environment Programme
UNFCCC	United Nations Framework Convention on Climate Change
USDA	United States Department of Agriculture
USGCRP	United States Global Change Research Program
WMO	World Meteorological Organization

References

Abrahamson, D.E. (1989). Global Warming: The Issues, Impacts, Responses. In D.E. Abrahamson (Ed.), *The Challenge of Global Warming*. Washington, DC: Island Press.

Adler, E. and P.M. Haas (1992). Conclusion: Epistemic Communities, World Order, and the Creation of a Reflective Research Program. *International Organization*, 46(1), 367–390.

Agence France-Presse (1999). Americans Begin to Worry about Genetically Modified Food. *New York Times*, June 21 (http://www.nytimes.com/library/national/science/health/062199hth-gm-food.html).

Allenby, Brad R. (2000). Earth Systems Engineering: The World as Human Artifact. *Bridge* 30(1), 5–13.

Alm, A. (1991). Why We Didn't Use "Risk" Before. *EPA Journal*, March/April.

Amara, R. (1991). Views on Futures Research Methodology. *Futures*, 23(6), 45–49.

Amato, I (1994). Crusade against Chlorine. *Garbage*, Summer, 24–39.

Arrhenius S. (1896). On the Influence of Carbonic Acid in the Air upon the Temperature of the Ground. *Philosophical Magazine*, 41, 237.

Arrow, K.J., M.L. Cropper, G.C. Eads, R.W. Hahn, L.B. Lave, R.G. Noll, P.R. Portney, M. Russell, R. Schmalensee, V.K. Smith, and R.N. Stavins (1996). Is There a Role for Benefit–Cost Analysis in Environmental, Health, and Safety Regulation? *Science*, 272, 221–222.

Associated Press (AP) (2000a). Developing a (Sort of) Chicken Soup for the Sickly Chicken. *New York Times*, January 18 (http://www.nytimes.com/library/national/science/011800sci-ge-chicken.html).

——— (2000b). Cloned Bulls Set to Be Dads. *New York Times*, March 24 (http://www.nytimes.com/aponline/i/AP-Japan-Cloning.html).

Baark, E. and J. Strahl (1995). The Response of International Organizations to the Environmental Challenge: The Case of the United Nations Industrial Development Organization (UNIDO). *Development and Change*, 26(3), 441–468.

Bamberger, Robert. (1993). Office interview, Former and Current: (202) 707-7240, Specialist in Energy Policy, Congressional Research Service, LM-423 Madison Building, Washington, DC 20540, 29 January.

Barboza, David (2000a). Modified Foods Put Companies in a Quandary. *New York Times*, June 4, 1.

———— (2000b). Suburban Genetics: Scientists Searching for a Perfect Lawn. *New York Times*, July 8. (http://www.nytimes.com/library/national/science/070900 grass-gm.html).

Bardach, E. (1977). *The Implementation Game: What Happens after a Bill Becomes a Law*. Cambridge, MA: MIT Press.

Baron, Richard (1999). An Assessment of Liability Rules for International GHG Emissions Trading. IEA Information Paper, October (http://ww.oecd/org/env/cc).

Benbrook, Charles (1993). Telephone interview, Former: Executive Director, Board on Agriculture, National Research Council, National Academy of Sciences. Current: (202) 546-5089, Benbrook Consulting, 409 First Street SE, Washington, DC 20003, 8 January.

Bender, Richard (1993). Office interview, Former and Current: (202) 224-7318, Legislative Aide, Senator Tom Harkin, Senate Hart Building, Room 531, Washington, DC 20510-1502, 16 February.

Blase, Melvin (1993). Telephone interview, Former and Current: (314) 882-0128, Dept. of Agricultural Economics, University of Missouri, Columbia, MO, 18 February.

Bressers, H., L.J. O'Toole Jr., and J. Richardson (1994). Networks as Models of Analysis: Water Policy in Comparative Perspective. *Environmental Politics*, 3(Winter), 1–23.

Brown, G.E., Jr. (1993). Science's Real Role in Policy-Making. *Chemical and Engineering News*, 71(22), 9–11.

Brown, Lester R., Michael Renner, and Brian Halweil (1999). *Vital Signs 1999: The Environmental Trends That Are Shaping Our Future*. New York, NY: W.W. Norton & Company.

———— (2000). *Vital Signs 2000: The Environmental Trends That Are Shaping Our Future*. New York, NY: W.W. Norton & Company.

Burros, Marian (1999). Documents Show Officials Disagreed on Altered Food. *New York Times*, December 1. (http://www.nytimes.com/library/national/science/120199sci-gm-foods.html).

Carley, M. (1980). *Rational Techniques in Policy Analysis*. Exeter, NH: Heinemann Educational.

Clark, W.C. (1991). Energy and Environment: Strategic Perspectives on Policy Design. In J.W. Tester, D.O. Wood, and N.A. Ferrari (Eds.), *Energy and the Environment in the 21st Century*, 63–78. Cambridge, MA: MIT Press.

Clark, William C. (1995). Environmental Intelligence. *Environment*. 37(7), separate page inside cover.

Clark, W.C. and G. Majone (1985). The Critical Appraisal of Scientific Inquiries with Policy Implications. *Science, Technology, and Human Values*, 10(3), 6–19.

Clinton Praises Bill Regulating Pesticide (1996). *New York Times*, August 4, 17.

Cohen, Roger. (1999). Fearful over the Future, Europe Seizes on Food. *New York Times*, August 29 (http://www.nytimes.com/library/review/ 082999europe-food-review.html).

Corliss, Mick (2000). U.S. Backs Kyoto Protocol in Theory, Not Promises. *Japan Times*, April 11.

Currie, Robert (1993). Personal communication, Associate Director, EPA Office of Strategic Planning, 3 March.

Daneke, G.A. (1992). Back to the Future: Misplaced Elements of Policy Inquiry and the Advanced Systems Agenda. In W.N. Dunn and R.M. Kelly (Eds.), *Advances in Policy Studies since 1950*. Policy Studies Review Annual, vol. 10. New Brunswick, NJ: Transaction Publishers.

Dao, James (2000). Acid Rain Law Found to Fail in Adirondacks. *New York Times*, March 27 (http://www.nytimes.com/library/national/science/032700sci-ny-environ.html).

Davis, P.A. (1992). Ancient Timber Protections Emerge from First Round. *Congressional Quarterly*, 9 May.

DeLeon, P. (1994a). Democracy and the Policy Sciences: Aspirations and Operations. *Policy Studies Journal*, 22(2), 200–212.

——— (1994b). The Policy Sciences Redux: New Roads to Post-Positivism. *Policy Studies Journal*, 22(1), 176–184.

——— (1994c). Reinventing the Policy Sciences: Three Steps Back to the Future. *Policy Sciences*, 27, 77–95.

Dittrich, Suzette. (1993). Telephone interview, Former: Professor Staff Member, Senate Subcommittee on Agricultural Research and General Legislation. Current: (202) 224-5207, Professional Staff Member, Senate Subcommittee on Agricultural Credit, Senate Russell Building, Room 328A, Washington DC 20510-6002, 29 February.

Doron, G. (1992). Rational Choice and the Policy Sciences. *Policy Studies Review*, 11(3–4), 359–369.

Dowding, K. (1995). Model or Metaphor? A Critical Review of the Policy Network Approach. *Political Studies*, 43, 136–158.

Dowlatabadi, H. (1995). Integrated Assessment Models of Climate Change: An Incomplete Overview. *Energy Policy*, 23(4–5), 289–296.

Dowlatabadi, H. and M.G. Morgan. (1993). A Model Framework for Integrated Studies of the Climate Problem. *Energy Policy*, 21(3), 209–221.

Dryzek, J.S. (1993). From Science to Argument. In F. Fisher and J. Forester (Eds.), *The Argumentative Turn in Policy Analysis and Planning*, 213–232). Durham, NC: Duke University Press.

Duke, J.A. (1983). *Handbook of Energy Crops*. (unpublished).(Available at http://www.hort.purdue.edu/newcrop/duke_energy/Helianthus_tuberosus.html).

Dunlap, Riley E., George H. Gallup Jr., and Alec M. Gallup (1993). *Health of the Planet.* Princeton, NJ: Gallup International Center.

Dunn, W.N. (1988). Methods of the Second Type: Coping with the Wilderness of Conventional Policy Analysis. *Policy Studies Review,* 7, 720–737.

————— (1994). *Public Policy Analysis: An Introduction.* 2nd ed. Englewood Cliffs, NJ: Prentice Hall.

Eberstadt, N. (1995). *The Tyranny of Numbers: Mismeasurement and Misrule.* La Vergne, TN: AEI Press.

Feder, Barnaby J. (1999). Plant Sterility Research Inflames Debate on Biotechnology's Role in Farming. *New York Times,* April 19 (http://www.nytimes.com/library/national/science/041999sci-agri-biotech.html).

Federal Facilities Environmental Restoration Dialogue Committee (FFERDC). (1993). *Interim Report. Recommendations for Improving the Federal Environmental Decision-Making and Priority-Setting Processes.* Washington, DC: U.S. EPA. Office of Federal Facilities Enforcement. Strategic Planning and Prevention Division. February.

Findeisen, W. and E.S. Quade (1985). The Methodology of Systems Analysis: An Introduction and Overview. In H.J. Miser and E.S. Quade (Eds.), *Handbook of Systems Analysis: Overview of Uses, Procedures, Applications, and Practice,* 117–149. New York: North-Holland.

Fischer, F. (1987). Policy Expertise and the "New Class": A Critique of the Neoconservative Thesis. In F. Fisher and J. Forester (Eds.), *Confronting Values in Policy Analysis,* 94–126. Beverly Hills, CA: Sage.

————— (1992). Participatory Expertise: Towards a Democratization of Policy Science. In W.N. Dunn and R.M. Kelly (Eds.), *Advances in Policy Studies since 1950,* 351–376. Policy Studies Review Annual, vol. 10. New Brunswick, NJ: Transaction Publishers.

————— (1993a). Citizen Participation and the Democratization of Policy Expertise: From Theoretical Inquiry to Practical Cases. *Policy Sciences,* 26, 165–187.

————— (1993b). Policy Discourse and the Politics of Washington Think Tanks. In F. Fisher and J. Forester (Eds.), *The Argumentative Turn in Policy Analysis and Planning.* Durham, NC: Duke University Press.

Foreman, C.T., and J. Harsch (1989). *Spreading the Word on Food and Farm Policy, Assessing the Policy Impact of the National Research Council's Board on Agriculture* (An assessment of the Board on Agriculture's policy impact completed at the request of the W.K. Kellogg Foundation, 30 September).

Forester, J. (1987). Anticipating Implementation: Normative Practices in Planning and Policy Analysis. In F. Fisher and J. Forester (Eds.), *Confronting Values in Policy Analysis,* 153–173. Beverly Hills, CA: Sage.

————— (1993). Learning from Practice Stories: The Priority of Practical Judgment. In F. Fisher and J. Forester (Eds.), *The Argumentative Turn in Policy Analysis and Planning,* 186–209. Durham, NC: Duke University Press.

Gilbert, G.R. (1984). The Study of Policy Formulation and the Conduct of Policy Analysis and Evaluation. In G.R. Gilbert (Ed.), *Making and Managing Policy: Formulation, Analysis, Evaluation*, 1–9. New York, NY: Marcel Dekker.

Gordon, John (1993). Personal communication, Dean, School of Forestry and Environmental Studies, Yale University, 23 March.

Gordon, T.J. (1992). The Methods of Futures Research. *Annals of the American Academy of Political and Social Science* 522, 25–35.

Govan, Emilia L. (1993). Personal communication, Senior Analyst, OTA, 21 May.

Haas, P.M. (1992a). Banning Chlorofluorocarbons: Epistemic Community Efforts to Protect Stratospheric Ozone. *International Organization*, 46(1), 187–224.

——— (1992b). Introduction: Epistemic Communities and International Policy Coordination. *International Organization*, 46(1), 1–35. Copyright 1992 by the World Peace Foundation and the Massachusetts Institute of Technology.

Heineman, R.A., W.T. Bluhm, S.A. Peterson, and E.N. Kearny (1990). *The World of the Policy Analyst: Rationality, Values, and Politics*. Chatham, NJ: Chatham House Publishers.

Hendrickson, C., L.B. Lave, and F. McMichael (1995). Reconsider Recycling. *Chemtech*, August, 56–60.

Hileman, B. (1993). Concerns Broaden over Chlorine and Chlorinated Hydrocarbons. *Chemical and Engineering News*, April 19, 11–20.

——— (1994). Report Says Chlorinated Organics Are Safe for Use. *Chemical and Engineering News*, August 29, 8.

Hileman, B., J.R. Long, and E.M. Kirschner (1994). Chlorine Industry Running Flat Out Despite Persistent Health Fears. *Chemical and Engineering News*, November 21, 12–26.

Hoge, Warren. (1999). Britons Skirmish over Genetically Modified Crops. *New York Times*, August 23 (http://www.nytimes.com/library/world/europe/082399sci-gm-britain.html).

Intergovernmental Panel on Climate Change (IPCC) (2000). About IPCC. (http://www.ipcc.ch/about/about.htm).

Jain, Ravi K. and Lloyd V. Urban (1998). Global Warming—Uncertainties, Effects, and Policy Options. *Environmental Engineering and Policy*, December, 87–95.

Jenkins-Smith, H.C. and P.A. Sabatier (1993). The Dynamics of Policy-Oriented Learning. In P.A. Sabatier and H.C. Jenkins-Smith (Eds.), *Policy Change and Learning: An Advocacy Coalition Approach*, 41–56. Boulder, CO: Westview Press.

Johnson, K.N., J.F. Franklin, J.W. Thomas, and J. Gordon. (The Scientific Panel on Late-Successional Forest Ecosystems) (1991). *Alternatives for Management of Late Successional Forests of the Pacific Northwest*. House of Representatives Report (Appendix III), 102-1039, October.

Kaiser, J. and M. Enserink (2000). Treaty Takes a POP at the Dirty Dozen. *Science*, 290, 2053.

Kenis, P. and V. Schneider (1991). Policy Networks and Policy Analysis: Scrutinizing a New Analytical Toolbox. In B. Marin and R. Mayntz (Eds.), *Policy Networks: Empirical Evidence and Theoretical Considerations*, 25–59. Boulder, CO: Westview Press.

Kirschner, E. (1994). Michigan Panel Rebuts Chlorine Ban Proposal. *Chemical and Engineering News*, July 11, 11.

Kiser, L.L. and E. Ostrom (1982). The Three Worlds of Action: A Metatheoretical Synthesis of Institutional Approaches. In E. Ostrom (Ed.), *Strategies of Political Inquiry*, 179–221. Beverly Hills, CA: Sage.

Klijn, E.H., J. Koppenjan, and K. Termee. (1995). Managing Networks in the Public Sector: A Theoretical Study of Management Strategies in Policy Networks. *Public Administration*, 73(3), 437–454.

Knott, J. and A. Wildavsky (1980). If Dissemination Is the Solution, What Is the Problem? *Knowledge: Creation, Diffusion, Utilization*, 1, 537–578.

Knox, Andrea (2000). Transgenic Animals Create Drugs at "Pharms." *Cincinnati Enquirer*, June 4, A8.

Lasswell, H.D. (1951). The Policy Orientation. In D. Lerner and H.D. Lasswell (Eds.), *The Policy Sciences*, 3–15. Stanford, CA: Stanford University Press.

Leggett, Jane (1993). Office interview, Former analyst, EPA Office of Policy Analysis. Current: (202) 260-8634, Chief, Climate Stabilization Branch, Office of Policy Analysis, EPA, 401 M St. SW, Washington, DC 20460, 28 January.

Lindblom, C. and D.K. Cohen (1979). *Usable Knowledge: Social Science and Social Problem Solving*. New Haven, CT: Yale University Press.

Loeber, A. (1996). Policy-Oriented Learning and the Role of Interactive Analysis: The STE Forum and Changes in the Eutrophication Policy in the Netherlands between 1970 and 1987. (Draft, unpublished paper).

Loehr, R. (1995). Looking Ahead to the Planet's Future. *EPA Journal*, 21, 22–25.

Lynn, L.E., Jr. (1987). *Managing Public Policy*. Boston: Little, Brown and Company.

Lyons, James R. (1993). Personal communication, Staff Assistant, Committee on Agriculture, U.S. House of Representatives, February.

Lyons, J.R. and J. Gordon (1993). Science, Scientists, and Policy in the Old-Growth Debate. Draft. Washington, DC: U.S. House of Representatives, Committee on Agriculture.

Manard, Rick (1993). Personal communication, Northeast Comprehensive Risk Reduction Center, Vermont, 16 March.

Marin, B. and R. Mayntz (1991). Introduction: Studying Policy Networks. In B. Marin and R. Mayntz (Eds.), *Policy Networks: Empirical Evidence and Theoretical Considerations*, 11–23. Boulder, CO: Westview Press.

McDonnell, L.M., and R.F. Elmore (1987). *Alternative Policy Instruments*. (JNE-03) Santa Monica, CA: Rand.

McGartland, Albert (1993). Personal communication, Director, EPA Office of Economic Analysis and Regulation, 10 March.

Mealey, Timothy (1993). Personal communication, Associate Director, The Keystone Center, March.

Moore, Jack (1993). Telephone interview, Former: Assistant Administrator of EPA for Pesticides and Toxic Substances. Current: (202) 289-8721, Director, Institute for Evaluating Health Risks, Suite 698, 1101 Vermont Ave. NW, Washington, DC 20005, 3 January.

Morgan, M.G., B. Fischhoff, A. Bostrom, L. Lave, and C.J. Atman (1992). Communicating Risk to the Public: First, Learn What People Know and Believe. *Environmental Science and Technology*, 26(11), 2048–2056.

Moynihan, Senator D.P. (1993). A Legislative Proposal. *EPA Journal*, Jan/Feb/Mar.

Myerson, Allen R. (1998). Monsanto Paying Delta Farmers to Settle Genetic Seed Complaints. *New York Times*, February 24 (http://www.nytimes.com/library/national/ science/022498monsanto-seed.html).

Nagel, S.S. (1980). *Improving Policy Analysis*. Beverly Hills, CA: Sage.

——— (1984). *Contemporary Public Policy Analysis*. Tuscaloosa: University of Alabama Press.

Narum, D. (1993). International Cooperation on Global Warming and the Rights of Future Generations. *Policy Sciences*, 26(1), 21–40.

National Research Council (NRC) (1987). *Regulating Pesticides in Food: The Delaney Paradox*. Washington, DC: National Academy Press.

——— (1999). *Global Environmental Change: Research Pathways for the Next Decade*. Washington, DC: National Academy Press.

Nichols, A. (1985). The Role of Analysis in Regulatory Decisions: The Case of Lead in Gasoline. (Unpublished paper, October).

Noronha, Frederick (1998). Persistent Organic Pollutants Pervade Asia. UNEP Press Release (http://www.chem.unep.ch/pops/POPs_Inc/press_releases/pressrel-99/pr13.htm).

O'Connell, Paul (1993). Telephone interview, Former: Special Assistant to USDA Assistant Secretary Orville Bentley. Current: (202) 401-4860, Director of AARC, U.S. Dept. of Agriculture, 14th and Independence Avenue, Cotton Annex, 2nd Floor Mezz., SW, Washington, DC 20250-0400, February 11.

Organization for Economic Cooperation and Development (OECD) (1999). International Emissions Trading Under the Kyoto Protocol. OECD Information Paper ENV/EPOC(99)18FINAL.

Oshima, S. and A. Murakami (1997). 160 Nations Adopt Kyoto Protocol. *Japan Times*, December 11.

Owens, Jim (1993). Personal communication, Ancient Forest Alliance, 11 March.

Ozawa, C. (1991). *Recasting Science: Consensual Procedures in Public Policy*. Boulder, CO: Westview Press.

Paehlke, R. and D. Torgerson (1992). Toxic Waste as Public Business. *Canadian Public Administration*, 35(3), 339–362.

Palumbo, Dennis J. (1992). Bucking the Tide: Policy Studies in Political Science, 1978–1988. In W.N. Dunn and R.M. Kelly (Eds.), *Advances in Policy Studies since 1950*, 59–80. Policy Studies Review Annual, vol. 10. New Brunswick, NJ: Transaction Publishers.

Palumbo, D.J. (1987). Politics and Evaluation. In D.J. Palumbo (Ed.), *The Politics of Program Evaluation*, 12–46. Beverly Hills, CA: Sage.

——— (1994). *Public Policy in America: Government in Action*. 2nd ed. Fort Worth, TX: Harcourt Brace College Publishers.

Parson, Edward A. and William C. Clark (1993). Sustainable Development as Social Learning: Theoretical Perspectives and Practical Challenges for the Design of a Research Program. Faculty Research Working Papers Series; John F. Kennedy School of Government Discussion Paper R93-37, November, 428–460. Cambridge, MA.

Patton, C.V. and D.S. Sawicki (1993). *Basic Methods of Policy Analysis and Planning*. Englewood Cliffs, NJ: Prentice Hall.

Patton, M.Q. (1987). Evaluation's Political Inherency: Practical Implications for Designs and Use. In D.J. Palumbo (Ed.), *The Politics of Program Evaluation*, 100–145. Beverly Hills, CA: Sage.

Petersen, Carol (1999). Biotech Expert's New Job Casts a Shadow on a Report. *New York Times*, August 16 (http://www.nytimes.com/library/national/science/081699sci-gm-report.html).

Phillips, Ian (2000). "Golden Rice" Free to Stem Blindness. *Cincinnati Enquirer*, May 17, A13.

Pollack, Andrew (2000a). With U.S. Under Pressure, Biotechnology Talks Resume. *New York Times*, January 23 (http://www.nytimes.com/library/world/global/012300biotech-us.html).

——— (2000b). Nations Agree on Safety Rules for Biotech Food. *New York Times*, January 30 (http://www.nytimes.com/library/national/science/013000scie-gm-treaty.html).

Quade, E.S. and G.M. Carter (1989). *Analysis for Public Decisions*. 3rd ed. Englewood Cliffs, NJ: Prentice Hall.

Raiffa, H. (1968). *Decision Analysis: Introductory Lectures on Choices under Uncertainty*. Menlo Park, CA: Addison-Wesley Publishing.

Reilly, W.K. (1991). Why I Propose a National Debate on Risk. *EPA Journal*, March/April.

Rein, M. (1976). *Social Science and Public Policy*. Baltimore, MD: Penguin Books.

Reuters (1999). Genetically Modified Food Headlines Frighten Public. *New York Times*, July 16 (http://www.nytimes.com/library/national/science/health/071699hth-gm-food.html).

Rissler, Jane and Margaret Mellon (1996). *The Ecological Risks of Engineered Crops*. Cambridge, MA: MIT Press.

Rubin, E.S., L.B. Lave, and M.G. Morgan (1992). Keeping Climate Research Relevant. *Issues in Science and Technology*, 8(2), 47–55.

Sabatier, P.A. and H.C. Jenkins-Smith (1993). *Policy Change and Learning: An Advocacy Coalition Approach.* Boulder, CO: Westview Press.

Schimek, P. and K. Merrigan (1994). *The Uses and Organization of Environmental Policy Studies.* (Prepared for the Army Environmental Policy Institute).

Schlager, E. (1995). Policy Making and Collective Action: Defining Coalitions within the Advocacy Coalition Framework. *Policy Sciences*, 28(3), 243–270.

Schniederjans, M.J. (1995). *Goal Programming: Methodology and Applications.* Boston: Kluwer Academic Publishers.

Schwartz, B., K.C. Bowen, I. Kiss, and E.S. Quade (1985). Guidance For Decisions. In H.J. Miser and E.S. Quade (Eds.), *Handbook of Systems Analysis: Overview of Uses, Procedures, Applications, and Practice*, 219–247. New York, NY: North-Holland.

Schwartz, Joel (1993). Office interview, Former and Current: (202) 260-2784, Senior Scientist, Office of Policy Analysis, EPA, 401 M St. SW, Washington, DC 20460, 29 January.

Schwartz, J., J. Leggett, B. Ostro, H. Pitcher, and R. Levin (1984). *Cost and Benefits of Reducing Lead in Gasoline.* Washington, DC: U.S. Environmental Protection Agency (draft final report).

Sebenius, J.K. (1992). Challenging Conventional Explanations of International Cooperation: Negotiation Analysis and the Case of Epistemic Communities. *International Organization*, 46(1), 323–365.

Shim, J.K., J.G. Siegel and C.J. Liew (1994). *Strategic Business Forecasting.* Chicago, IL: Probus Publishing Company.

Socolow, R. (1997). Fuel Decarbonization and Carbon Sequestration: Report of A Workshop (report no. 302). Princeton, NJ: Princeton University Center for Energy and Environmental Studies.

Spencer, Peter (1999). Biotech Foods: Right to Know What? *Consumers' Research*, October 10, 10–43.

Susskind, L.E. (1994). *Environmental Diplomacy: Negotiating More Effective Global Agreements.* New York: Oxford University Press.

Susskind, L. and J. Cruikshank (1987). *Breaking the Impasse: Consensual Approaches to Resolving Public Disputes.* New York, NY: Basic Books.

Susskind, L.E. and M. Elliott (1983). *Paternalism, Conflict and Coproduction: Learning From Citizen Action and Citizen Participation in Western Europe.* New York: Plenum Press.

Susskind, L. and P. Field (1996). *Dealing with an Angry Public.* New York: Free Press.

Susskind, L. and D. Laws (1994). Siting Solid Waste Facilities in the United States. In F. Kreith (Ed.), *Handbook of Solid Waste Management*, 13.1–13.15. New York: McGraw-Hill, Inc.

Susskind, L.E., S. McKearnan, and J. Thomas-Larmer, (1999). *The Consensus Building Handbook: A Comprehensive Guide to Reaching Agreement.* Thousand Oaks, CA: Sage.

Taylor, Robert E. (1995). What's Wrong with Chlorine? *Safety & Health,* July, 70–74.

Thies, Greg (1993). Office visit, Former: U.S. Senate Agricultural Committee minority professional staff member responsible for pesticide issues. Current: (513) 644-0011, Director of Government Relations, The O.M. Scott & Sons Company, 14310 Scottslawn Road, Marysville, OH 43041, 7 January.

Toman, Michael and Marina Cazorla (1998). The Clean Development Mechanism: A Primer. *Weathervane,* September 29 (http://www.weathervane.rff.org/features/feature048.html).

Toren, K. and P.D. Blanc (1997). The History of Pulp and Paper Bleaching: Respiratory-Health Effects. *Lancet,* May 3, 1316–1318.

United Nations Environment Programme (UNEP) (2000). Progress Made in Negotiating Global Treaty on Persistent Organic Pollutants; 121 Countries Participate. UNEP News Release (http://irptc.unep.ch/pops/POPs_Inc/press-releases/pressrel-2k/prmarch27.htm).

U.S. Congress (1988). Statement of Senator Kent Conrad on S. 2413. *Congressional Record,* 134(71), May 19.

———— OTA (1991). *Complex Cleanup: The Environmental Legacy of Nuclear Weapons Production.* (OTA-O-484) February.

———— (1995). Statement of Senator Daniel Patrick Moynihan on S. 123. *Congressional Record,* 141, January 4.

———— (1998). Hearing on the Impact and Status of the Northern Spotted Owl on National Forests: Oversight Hearing before the Subcommittee on Forests and Forest Health of the Committee on Resources, House of Representatives, March 19, 1998 (http://commdocs.house.gov/committees/resources/ hii47909.000/hii47909_0f.htm).

———— GAO (2000). *Acid Rain: Emissions Trends and Effects in the Eastern United States.* (GAO/RECED-00-47) March.

U.S. Department of Agriculture, New Farm and Forest Products Task Force (1987). *New Farm and Forest Products: Responses to the Challenges and Opportunities Facing American Agriculture.* Washington, DC: USDA (June 25).

U.S. Environmental Protection Agency (U.S. EPA) (1990). *Reducing Risk: Setting Priorities and Strategies for Environmental Protection.* (SAB-EC-90-021) Washington, DC: U.S. EPA (September).

———— (1995a). *Beyond the Horizon: Using Foresight to Protect the Environmental Future.* (EPA-SAB-EC-95-007). Washington, DC: U.S. EPA.

———— (1995b). *SAB Report: Futures Methods and Issues (A Technical Annex to "Beyond the Horizon: Protecting the Future with Foresight."* (EPA-SAB-EC-95-007A) Washington, DC: U.S. EPA.

———— (1999a). International Emissions Trading: The U.S. View—October 1999. EPA Factsheet (http://www.epa.gov/globalwarming/publications/actions/cop5/intl_trading.html).

———— (1999b). The Clean Development Mechanism: The U.S. View—October 1999. EPA Factsheet (http://www.epa.gov/globalwarming/publications/actions/cop5/cdm_99.html).

U.S. Fish and Wildlife Service (1996). *An Environmental Alternatives Analysis for a 4(d) Rule for the Northern Spotted Owl.* Portland, OR: U.S. Fish and Wildlife Service.

Vickers, G. (1995). *The Art of Judgment: A Study of Policy Making.* Thousand Oaks, CA: Sage.

Walker, W.E. and G.H. Fisher (1994). *Public Policy Analysis: A Brief Definition.* (P-7856) Santa Monica, CA: Rand.

Webber, D.J. (1992). The Distribution and Use of Policy Knowledge in the Policy Process. In W.N. Dunn and R.M. Kelly (Eds.), *Advances in Policy Studies since 1950.* Policy Studies Review Annual, vol. 10. New Brunswick, NJ: Transaction Publishers.

Weimer, D.L. (1992). The Craft of Policy Design: Can It Be More Than Art? *Policy Studies Review,* 11(3–4), 370–398.

Weimer, D.L. and A.R. Vining (1989). *Policy Analysis: Concepts and Practice.* Englewood Cliffs, NJ: Prentice Hall.

Weiss, C.H. (1978). The Many Meanings of Research Utilization. *Public Administration Review,* 39, 426–431.

———— (1989). Improving the Linkage between Research and Public Policy. In L. Lynn, Jr. (Ed.), *Knowledge and Policy: The Uncertain Connection.* Washington, DC: National Academy Press.

White, Gilbert F., William C. Clark, Alan McGowan, and Timothy O'Riordan (1992). Taking Stock of UNCED. *Environment,* 34(8), 506–525.

White, L.G. (1994). Policy Analysis as Discourse. *Journal of Policy Analysis and Management,* 13(3), 506–525.

White, R.M. (1993). Introduction: Environmental Regulation and Changing Science and Technology. In M.F. Uman (Ed.), *Keeping Pace with Science and Engineering: Case Studies in Environmental Regulation,* 1–7. Washington, DC: National Academy Press.

Wildavsky, A. (1987). *Speaking Truth to Power.* 2nd ed. New Brunswick, NJ: Transactions Publishers.

Wiles, Richard (1993). Telephone interview, Former: Project Officer, Board on Agriculture, National Research Council, National Academy of Sciences. Current: (202) 667-6982, Director of the Agricultural Pollution Prevention Project, Center for Resource Economics, 1718 Connecticut Avenue, Suite 201 NW, Washington, DC 20009, 26 January.

Williams, B.R. (1987). *Making Research Useful to Policymakers*. (P-7386) Santa Monica, CA: Rand.

Witter, Willis (1997). Greenhouse-Gas Accord is Reached in Kyoto. *Washington Times*, December 11.

Yoon, Carol Kaesuk (1999a). Pollen from Genetically Altered Corn Threatens Monarch Butterfly, Study Finds. *New York Times*, May 20 (http://www.nytimes.com/library/national/science/052099sci-butterfly-danger.html).

——— (1999b). New Federal Checks Exist on the Growing of Crops Whose Genes Are Altered. *New York Times*, November 3 (http://www. nytimes.com/library/national/science/110399sci-ge-squash.html).

——— (2000a). E.P.A. Announces New Rules on Genetically Altered Corn. *New York Times*, January 17 (http://www.nytimes.com/library/national/science/011700sci-ge-crop.html).

——— (2000b). Type of Biotech Corn Found to Be Safe to a Butterfly Species. *New York Times*, June 6 (http://www.nytimes.com/library/national/science/060600sci-gm-corn.html).

——— (2000c). A Call for Biotechnology to Be Used for the Developing World. *New York Times*, July 11 (http://www.nytimes.com/library/national/science/071100sci-gm-farming.html).

Yosie, T.F. (1996). The Changing Landscape of the Chlorine Debate. *Environmental Science and Technology*, November, 498A–501A.

About the Authors

LAWRENCE E. SUSSKIND is Ford Professor of Urban and Environmental Planning at the Massachusetts Institute of Technology where he has served as a member of the faculty for 30 years. Professor Susskind received his B.A. from Columbia University and his master of city planning and Ph.D. in urban and regional planning from MIT. At MIT, Professor Susskind is head of the Environmental Policy Group and director of the Environmental Technology and Public Policy Program in the Department of Urban Studies and Planning.

Professor Susskind served as the first executive director of the Program on Negotiation (PON) at Harvard Law School and is current director of the MIT–Harvard Public Disputes Program at PON. In that capacity he has served as editor of the annual *Papers on International Environmental Negotiation* and was founder and editor of *The Environmental Impact Assessment Review* for almost 20 years.

Since 1993, Professor Susskind has served as president of the Consensus Building Institute, a not-for-profit organization that provides dispute resolution services in complex public disputes around the world. He has served as a special master and mediator of more than 50 multi-party, multi-issue disputes and has helped to pioneer the field of environmental dispute resolution in the United States and Europe. He is the author of more than 100 book chapters, technical reports, and articles as well as 14 books including *Breaking the Impasse: Consensual Approaches to Resolving Public Disputes* (with Jeffrey Cruikshank), *Environmental Diplomacy, Dealing with an Angry Public* (with Patrick Field), *Negotiating Better Environmental Agreements* (with Paul Levy and Jennifer Thomas-Larmer), and *The Consensus Building Handbook* (with Sarah McKearnan and Jennifer Thomas-Larmer).

RAVI K. JAIN is Dean of the School of Engineering and Professor of Engineering at the University of the Pacific, Stockton, California. He received his B.S. and M.S. degrees in civil engineering from California State University and a Ph.D. in civil engineering from Texas Tech. He studied public administration and public policy at Harvard, earning an M.P.A. degree.

Prior to this appointment, Professor Jain has been an Associate Dean for Research and International Engineering and Executive Director of Interdisciplinary Research Centers, professor of civil engineering and environmental engineering, and director of the Environmental Engineering Management Graduate Program at the University of Cincinnati, College of Engineering.

He has held research and faculty appointments at the University of Illinois (Urbana-Champaign) and Massachusetts Institute of Technology. He has been a Littauer Fellow at Harvard University and a Fellow at Churchill College at Cambridge University.

He has directed a staff of over 200 engineers and scientists, conducting interdisciplinary research for the U.S. Army, and was the Founding Director of the Army Environmental Policy Institute (AEPI). He has worked for the California State Department of Water Resources and Industry and has been a consultant to federal agencies, international organizations and private industry and has provided expert testimony concerning environmental engineering and environmental policy related issues.

Professor Jain has served on numerous National Task Forces and Advisory Councils for the Department of Defense, NSF, Navy, Army, EPA, and NAS. He is a fellow ASCE and Diplomate American Academy of Environmental Engineers.

Professor Jain is the author of more than 100 journal articles, technical papers, and book chapters as well as 12 books, including *Management of Research and Development Organizations: Managing the Unmanageable* (with Harry Triandis) and *Environmental Assessment* (with Lloyd Urban, Gary Stacey, and Harold Balbach). He is Editor-In-Chief of the international journal *Environmental Engineering and Policy*.

ANDREW O. MARTYNIUK is assistant director of the Center for Environmental Assessment and Policy, University of Cincinnati College of Engineering. He received a B.S. degree from Cornell University in engineering and geological sciences, an M.S. in systems management from the University of Southern California, and a J.D. from the University of Cincinnati College of Law. He is a member of the Ohio Bar and the Patent Bar. His current research interests include intellectual property law, environmental law and policy, and technology transfer.

Index

O'Connell, Paul, 52, 53, 54, 55
Office of Strategic Planning, EPA, 46, 47
Office of Technology Assessment (OTA),
    69, 125; *Complex Cleanup* study
    conducted by, 39, 39–40, 69, 71, 77, 78;
    Oceans and Environment Program, 40
Oil refineries, 32. See also *Lead in Gasoline*
    study
Omnibus farm bill (1990), 51
Open forums, 122
Operations research (OR), 91–93
Options, policy. *See* Policy
    recommendations
Organizational auspices, 65, 76–77, 87, 135
Organizational arrangements, 29, 78, 97
Organizational constraints. *See*
    Institutional constraints
OR (operations research), 91–93
OTA. *See* Office of Technology Assessment
    (OTA)
O'Toole, L.J., Jr., 104, 106
Owens, Jim, 76
Ozawa, C., 122, 124

Paehlke, R. and D. Torgerson, 102
Parallel research efforts, 68
Paris Commission on Land Based Sources
    of Pollution to the North Atlantic, 130
Parson, Edward A. and William C. Clark,
    153
Participatory policy analysis, 100–101, 102,
    104, 121
Patton, C.V., 8, 11
PCBs (polychlorinated biphenyls), 1, 131
Peer review process, 77–78, 87; credibility
    and, 65, 116; faulty data and, 85; in the
    Lead in Gasoline study, 33, 69
Persistent organic pollutants (POPs), 131;
    treaties to eliminate, 131–32. *See also*
    Chlorinated organic compounds
Pesticide-resistant crops, 148
Pesticides: children's health risks and, 27, 33;
    in foods, 20–22, 24–25, 26, 30, 115; POPs
    in, 131. See also *Delaney Paradox* study
Peterson, Carol, 150

Pharmaceuticals (genetically engineered),
    152
Phillips, Ian, 146
Plant breeding, 145. *See also* Transgenic
    crops
Policy actors, 105, 106, 109; decision
    makers, 14, 19, 96, 97
Policy analysis: analytical methods, 6, 74,
    113–16, 135; as a client-centered
    relationship, 101–2; defined, 6, 90–91,
    98; evaluation component, 10, 11,
    77–78, 85–86, 127; the evolution of
    policy science, 89–91, 111–12; follow-up
    procedures in, 81–82; future factors
    considered in, 79, 95, 127; methods of,
    87, 90–93, 119, 135–36; political context
    of, 75, 97–100; process methods, 6, 135;
    "real time" documentation in, 81;
    relevant information to, 11–12;
    rhetorical methods, 6, 116–17, 135;
    systems analysis in, 91, 93f., 93–95. *See
    also* Environmental policy studies;
    Experts; Organizational auspices; Policy
    recommendations
Policy analysis errors: erroneous
    recommendations, 84–85; rigged or
    biased studies, 14–15
Policy innovation, 110–11. *See also*
    Reframing issues
Policy instruments, 126–27
Policy learning, 80, 87, 107, 108, 122, 135;
    cross-case analysis, 80–81
Policy network analysis, 104, 104–7, 105–6,
    107
Policy recommendations: *Complex Cleanup*
    study recommendations, 41, 42, 43, 45,
    125; *Delaney Paradox* study
    recommendations, 28; *Lead in Gasoline*
    study recommendations, 36; presenting
    a range of policy options, 4–5, 10, 11,
    19–20; ranking alternatives, 94–95;
    Reducing Risk study recommendations,
    47; ruling out opposing arguments, 37.
    See also Credibility; Peer review process
Politics: as context of policy analysis, 75,

Island Press Board of Directors

Chair
HENRY REATH
President, Collector's Reprints, Inc.

Vice-Chair
VICTOR M. SHER
Environmental Lawyer

Secretary
DANE NICHOLS
Chairman, The Natural Step, U.S.

Treasurer
DRUMMOND PIKE
President, The Tides Foundation

WILLIAM M. BACKER
Backer, Spielvogel, Bates (ret.)

ROBERT E. BAENSCH
Professor of Publishing,
New York University

MABEL H. CABOT

DAVID C. COLE
Sunnyside Farms, LLC

CATHERINE M. CONOVER

GENE E. LIKENS
Director,
The Institute of Ecosystem Studies

CAROLYN PEACHEY
Campbell Peachey & Associates

WILL ROGERS
Trust for Public Lands

CHARLES C. SAVITT
President, Center for Resource
Economics/Island Press

SUSAN E. SECHLER
Director of Global Programs,
The Rockefeller Foundation

PETER R. STEIN
Managing Partner,
The Lyme Timber Company

RICHARD TRUDELL
Executive Director, American Indian
Resources Institute

WREN WIRTH
President, The Winslow Foundation